Dear Christy,
    If you can
the 1st 2 years of Nursing,
do Anything! Hang in there!
    Enjoy the Angels,

Karen
Brown

Among
The
Angels

CHRISTY —
You are a fine
teacher Hang in there
Best
[signature]

Among The *Angels*

Stories From Kindergarten

WILLIAM L. BROWN

authorHOUSE®

AuthorHouse™
1663 Liberty Drive
Bloomington, IN 47403
www.authorhouse.com
Phone: 1-800-839-8640

Published by AuthorHouse   12/22/2014

ISBN: 978-1-4817-4008-1 (sc)
ISBN: 978-1-4817-4007-4 (hc)
ISBN: 978-1-4817-4006-7 (e)

Library of Congress Control Number: 2013906636

To Karen, Carl, Irene and the Angels

And in memory of mother, Mary Elizabeth Schwertley Brown,
a glorious teacher, *requiescat in pace*

"Above all, *love little children, for they are sinless like the angels, and they are there to arouse our tenderness, to purify our hearts and in a sense to guide us.*"[1]

---

[1]   Fyodor Dostoyevsky, *The Brothers Karamazov*, translated by Andrew R. MacAndrew, p.386 Bantam Books (1970).

Contents

Introduction

"What are you doing today?" I innocently asked.

"The Gingerbread Man," Karen cheerfully replied.

That answer germinated the idea for this book.

We were both standing before mirrors, getting ready for work. I was in the bedroom, attempting to tie my tie, and Karen was in the bathroom, fixing into a ponytail her long, curly blonde hair.

My question was a casual one, but the answer stunned me. That day I was due in family law court for an ugly child custody trial, with allegations of incest and spousal abuse, before a judge who seldom deigned to digest the pleadings, a treacherous opposing counsel, an honest, but obtuse client, and an opposing party practiced in deceit.

It was the fall of 1994. Karen and I had been married for only two weeks. We had just moved into our new home perched on the edge of a mesa, with a dazzling westward view that swept from the farmland 200 feet below, to the dunes and settled on the Pacific Ocean. Through our rear wall of sheeted glass, we beheld, arrayed over the valley floor a thousand acres of alluvial soil, arranged into scores of contiguous rectangular plots, constantly ripped, disked, laser leveled, plowed, planted, irrigated, pruned and harvested, producing in rotating segments, crops of celery, cauliflower, lettuce and broccoli, forming an ever-changing earthen quilt in hues of black, charcoal, brown, tan, and every shade of green; bounded on the west by a wall of pristine dunes, 100 feet high, edging the cobalt sea, into which the burnished globe of the setting sun nightly dipped and disappeared with a final burst of light.

Karen and I had met in 1993, only ten months earlier. We had both recently ended long-term marriages of twenty years. Both of our former spouses had, more or less, walked away.

Karen had been a kindergarten teacher since 1975, all but the first year spent in Room 1 at Grover Beach Elementary School.

Since 1986, I had been in my second career as a lawyer. My earlier career had been as a professional tennis player inside the world's top 100 players, but otherwise of little note. Though privileged to have played against Laver, Emerson, Newcombe, Ashe, Connors, Smith, Nastase, and Borg in the great venues of the game in France (at Rolland Garros), England (at Wimbledon), the United States (at Forest Hills) and Australia (at Kooyong); I had merely been able "[t]o swell a progress, start a scene or two."[2] In the firmament lit by the most brilliant stars of the game, I was but a dim and distant light.

---

[2]   T.S. Eliot, *The Wasteland and Other Writings*, p. 7, The Love Song of J. Alfred Prufrock, The Modern Library Paperback Edition (2002).

About a week later, over breakfast, I again asked Karen: "What are you doing today?"

"Brown Bear, Brown Bear," she sweetly replied.

I immediately again reflected upon what appeared to be the beauty of her professional life, and the relative ugliness of mine, as once again I was off to court for more family law hearings full of high drama and low behavior.

Four months later, in January of 1995, I first visited Karen and the angels, and experienced my first indelible kindergarten moment.

In the poem *Among School Children* by William Butler Yeats, the speaker, while visiting a classroom, described himself as "[a] sixty-year-old smiling public man."[3]

I was a 50-year-old, seldom-smiling lawyer. I had finished with court early that day, as my cases had all been continued. I decided I needed to visit the classroom and see Karen and the angels.

I arrived unannounced at 11:00 a.m. When I opened the door, I looked to my right to see Karen speaking to the angels, assembled on the carpet in front of her. Carl

---

[3] *The Collected Poems of W. B. Yeats,* Edited by Richard J. Finneran, Among School Children, p. 216, Revised Second Edition, Scribner Paperback Poetry, Simon& Schuster (1996).

Daughters, Karen's team teaching partner, was in the back of the room, working on some of the classroom's computers.

When Karen saw me, she was surprised, but immediately turned my visit into the excitement of a guessing game.

In that animated and exaggerated way that I came to understand was Karen's way of getting and maintaining the angels' rapt attention, her voice rising, she asked, "Well, we have a visitor today. Who could this be?"

I took a few steps forward around the shelves of toys so that the angels, arrayed in four parallel rows on the carpet, could better behold me. They saw a graying man, 6'3-1/2" tall, weighing 200 pounds, peering through gold, horn-rimmed glasses, wrapped in a dark blue suit, a crisp, natural collar, white shirt, punctuated by a solid, cherry-red tie, standing in black, tasseled loafers.

Karen again asked the angels for guesses as to my identity. "Who could this be?"

It was soon to become apparent that the angels' all-too-frequent experiences tangent to the criminal justice system affected their guesses.

Small hands were raised. Karen called on a girl in the middle of the third row. "Is he a police officer, Mrs. Brown?"

"No, he is not a police officer," answered Karen.

Karen called on another raised hand, a boy in the second row. "Is he a judge?"

"No, he is not a judge," said Karen.

Karen called on a boy in the first row. "Is he your probation officer, Mrs. Brown?" Karen and I exchanged a quick glance.

"No, Mrs. Brown does not have a probation officer," answered Karen.

A girl in the fourth row had been excitingly waving her hand. Karen called on her. "I know! It's Martin Luther King, Jr.!"

Karen, Carl and I all exchanged quick glances.

There was one black angel in the class, a boy who immediately began wildly waving his hand. I thought the boy would point out the obvious. I am white. Martin Luther King, Jr. was black. Karen called on him.

The little boy emphatically said: "That can't be Martin Luther King, Jr. He's dead!"

Karen stopped the guessing at that point and introduced me to the assembled as "Mr. Brown . . . my husband . . . the daddy in my house."

This seemed to confuse a number of the angels, as they had assumed that Karen and Carl Daughters, her team teaching partner, were husband and wife. Yet, as the morning class left for the day, three girl angels hugged me as they left. Apparently, my mere association with Karen caused them to trust me enough to do that.

At home that night, I asked Karen why she thought the little girl guessed the way she did, and why the little black boy answered the way he did.

"They don't see color. They only see the person. And I had a small photo of Martin Luther King, Jr. behind me on the front wall, showing him in a dark suit and red tie. I was just starting to talk about Dr. King, because the national holiday bearing his name was coming up," she answered.

That was the first truth I learned from Karen about the angels. "They don't see color—only the person."

The second truth was how trusting and loving the angels were, and thus the hugs given to me.

In contrast, I told Karen that in eight years of representing mostly female clients, some of whom I had managed to make independently wealthy for life, few had said thanks, and none had ever hugged me.

As the days passed, after Karen came home, I asked her what had happened that day in kindergarten. She began to relate the most beautiful and heartwarming stories about the little angels in her care.

I began to make notes about those stories, and for the next 14 years stored those notes throughout the house.

By August of 2008, I had given myself permission to leave the caustic cauldron of the law. Karen's positive influence upon me helped me to see that no matter how lucrative, I was living a toxic professional life that left me constantly riven with rage.

So I helped Karen set up the classroom and commenced daily visits to Karen's kindergarten. I felt I could not write about Karen and kindergarten unless I better and truly understood both. So, I volunteered in Karen's kindergarten for the academic years 2008-2011, up to the moment of Karen's final day, on Friday, June 10, 2011. She officially retired from teaching on the following day.

Except for those periods of time when I was at home caring full time for my own children when they were toddlers, it was the most beautiful time of my life.

In that time, I confirmed Karen's beatific nature, the brilliance of her teaching, and the beauty of the angels in her care.

The following stories are what I heard from Karen, or experienced myself, as I learned about Karen, the angels, and kindergarten.

But first, I must describe the players, the setting, the scene, and the schedule.

I'm So Special...

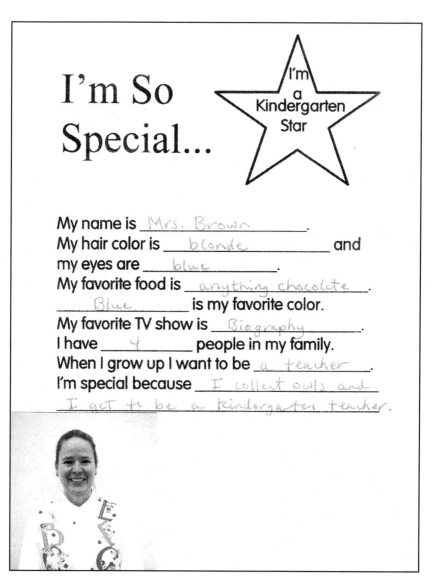

I'm a Kindergarten Star

My name is _Mrs. Brown_.
My hair color is _blonde_ and
my eyes are _blue_.
My favorite food is _anything chocolate_.
Blue is my favorite color.
My favorite TV show is _Biography_.
I have _4_ people in my family.
When I grow up I want to be _a teacher_.
I'm special because _I collect owls and I get to be a kindergarten teacher_.

Karen-a Kindergarten Star

Karen

Two ironies bracket Karen's professional life among the 1,000 angels she loved and taught over her 36-year kindergarten career. One, as a little girl, she never completed her own kindergarten. Two, as a woman, she never gave birth to her own children.

Four years old in September, Karen's mid-December birthday disqualified her from attending public school kindergarten. She would have to have turned age 5 by December 1st. Since Karen already knew colors, shapes, letters, numbers, days of the week, how to count, and to read small books, Karen's mother, Dolores, enrolled her into a nearby private kindergarten, so near to her San Bernardino home, that she could walk to school. After about two weeks, the kindergarten teacher held a conference with Dolores, suggesting that Karen should be advanced to 1st grade, since she already knew so much and was emotionally mature. Thus, Karen was moved to 1st grade, after only a glimpse of kindergarten.

This was at a time when kindergarten was pure fun. It wasn't until 40 years later that misguided educators perceived the procrustean notion of cramming into kindergarten much of the 1st grade curriculum.

As a woman, Karen became a teacher so that her vacations would mirror those of her future children. Only after that decision did she learn that a defect in her liver prevented her from ever giving birth.

I met Karen on December 7, 1993. I knew within moments that I was in the presence of goodness. We were never apart from that day and were married on September 17, 1994. During that time I learned from Karen that she had been born in Albuquerque, New Mexico and moved, at the age of two, to Rialto in San Bernardino County, then, after a year, to city of San Bernardino.

When Karen was 14, her family moved to Huntington Beach. There Karen could traverse a tomato field behind her house and go directly across Highway 1, the Pacific Coast Highway, to Bolsa Chica Beach, northern neighbor to the contiguous Huntington Beach, home of the surfer culture, immortalized by the Beach Boys.

By the time Karen left for college, she had enjoyed three quintessential California experiences.

One, while living in San Bernardino, she had eaten at the original McDonald's brother's fast-food burger joint.

Two, she graced the local surfer culture with her stunning face, long blond hair, and fabulous figure. She turned a lot of heads. Even her PE class at Huntington High was surfing! When I tell this to my Nebraska childhood friends, and to my Iowa relatives, who still farm the family farms, they, like me, are incredulous.

Three, she worked briefly at Disneyland and met Walt Disney.

A stellar student, Karen graduated from California Polytechnic State University at San Luis Obispo with a degree in social work. After working at an Orange County bank to pay off student loans, Karen earned her elementary teaching credential. When her husband, Bob, an aeronautical engineer, took a job at the Diablo Canyon nuclear power plant, at Avila Beach in San Luis Obispo county, Karen initially got hired at Nipomo Elementary as a credentialed reading aide.

The following year Karen got her first classroom as a kindergarten teacher at the bucolic Branch Elementary School in rural Arroyo Grande. Elevated on the slope of a hillside, above the irrigated farmlands of the narrow Huasna Valley, the school had a distant view to the sea and was surrounded by pastureland. There is where Karen met cows and the cowgirl.

The cows, Black Angus steers, would often wander onto the school grounds and Karen, all of 105 pounds when soaking wet, would futilely try to shoo them off. The 1,000-pound steers, lazily lifted their heads in her direction, and then languidly resumed chewing the fresh grass. The rancher would soon show up, laugh at Karen, and then simply bark a command to the cattle, which thundered back behind the appropriate fences.

The cowgirl was four years old when she started kindergarten. She had a mother who would drive her to school from their nearby acreage, but in the spring, the self-reliant cowgirl insisted on riding to and from school-bareback on her own horse. With the rancher's permission she left her horse in a pasture next to the school (the same one the cattle usually escaped from), and at the end of the day would go to the fence line and call out for her horse, who would walk over to her. She then opened the gate. The horse would pass, stop, and wait till the cowgirl closed the gate. Then she grabbed the horse's mane with both hands, jumped onto the horse, and rode off.

Karen cried the first three months of her kindergarten career, as the work was so hard. But, thanks be to God, she stuck with it. At the end of that first year, Karen heard about a new reading program, HEP (the Hawaii English Project), to be used at several select schools in the district, including Grover City. She took training classes that next summer and was hired at Grover City Elementary in fall 1976. She arrived at Room 1 and stayed there for the next 36 years, earning, along the way, a master's degree in early childhood education.

When I met Karen, she was in the full flower of her kindergarten career. When we married and moved in together in the fall of 1994, I began to glimpse the full beauty of Karen, and of her world through various revelations.

First, I noticed how happily Karen left for work each day. She was so cheerful, her blond ponytail bobbing down the hallway to the garage as she left for work. And she left so early. She did not need to be on campus until 8:00 a.m., but she got there at 6:55 or earlier on most days. She was always the first teacher there. That extra hour amounted to at least an extra 180 hours per the 180 school days per year, or about an extra 22.5 days. Over Karen's 36 years at Grover Beach, that amounted to an extra 810 days, an extra 4.5 years of uncompensated time.

Next, I began to notice Karen's wardrobe. She had a sweater, a blouse, or a t-shirt, and matching socks for each theme she was stressing in the classroom. The first week she wore various items of Gingerbread Man clothing. The second week she started wearing Brown Bear outfits. Then Columbus Day, then generic fall colors, then came Thanksgiving, then Christmas. Karen had so many different Christmas outfits, I don't know how she was able to store them, or find them. Then there was President's Day, and Valentine's Day, and St. Patrick's Day, and Easter, and owl outfits when Karen did her owl unit, and Hawaiian outfits when she did her Hawaiian unit.

Then, in early October, I noticed a new tablecloth appeared from nowhere in fall hues of red and orange, accompanied by a centerpiece of fall leaves. On Columbus Day, a themed centerpiece appeared on the dining room table, and a matching tablecloth. Thanksgiving was more elaborate, with turkey centerpieces, hand towels in the

5

guest bathroom, turkey tablecloths, etc. But Christmas was the extravaganza. I would carry from the garage, ten great plastic storage tubs and turn Karen loose. The heaviest tub contained only Christmas snow globes. Another contained only owl ornaments. Another held nothing but crèches. Another held Christmas hand towels. Another held Christmas wall decorations. Another held only Christmas lights. Much living room furniture had to be moved. The tree had to be purchased and set up. Every room in the house boasted something of the Christmas season when Karen was done.

Special household decorations also appeared on: Presidents' Day; Valentine's' Day; St. Patrick's Day; Easter; Memorial Day; and July 4th.

Fourteen years later, when I started daily going to Karen's kindergarten, I soon realized that what seasonal decorating Karen did around the house was nothing when compared to the elaborate and constantly changing decorations in her classroom.

Eventually, I came to see that Karen shared much with the angels in her care.

The angels are open to everybody, and so was Karen. The phone rang off the hook for her. I had few friends and fewer close acquaintances. I seldom received a phone call. Karen had not a friend to spare. Everybody wanted Karen . . . to be with her, to speak to her, to plan to do things with her. Calls would come from: the PEO; the Lions Club; Delta Kappa Gamma; a fellow teacher; a former teacher; an old friend; a current friend; a parent; a former parent; or a relative. Karen cherished friendships as well as acquaintances. The disparity between phone calls received soon became so obvious between us, that for years a running remark I have been making to Karen after I have been called by someone, usually my mother, brother, or sisters, is: "See . . . I have friends."

Like the angels, Karen did not see the color of a person's skin. Many times Karen and I have met or spoken to a person of color and later I will realize that Karen did not know, or did not notice, that they were African American, or Mexican, or Oriental.

Like the angels, Karen is utterly unthreatening and disarming. Karen strikes up conversations everywhere with anyone. We will be standing in the check out line of a department store. I will nod to the lady behind me. Karen then strikes up a conversation, which soon becomes animated and continues even after I have paid and we are leaving the counter. Eventually, I pull Karen away and we leave. When we get into the car, Karen then excitedly tells me all about the woman I had nodded to: her place of birth, number and location of siblings, marital and medical history, including completed and impending procedures, vacation plans and other predilections, hopes, regrets, and a pressing personal problem or two. I am no longer amazed at this.

Like the angels, Karen abhors violence. Karen never sees a violent movie or television program. If a violent image appears unexpectedly on the television screen, she changes the channel, or covers her eyes. Thus, the producers of movies seldom offer anything that appeals to Karen, and she seldom sees a movie, though she did see *Mary Poppins* and *The Sound Of Music,* and sees an occasional Disney offering. Clint Eastwood's oeuvre is unknown to her, so also are that of Charles Bronson, Sylvester Stallone, Arnold Schwarzenegger, etc. If I want to watch *Dirty Harry,* I do so out of Karen's sight and sound. The same holds true of television, which offers little tolerable for Karen, except comedies and the Home and Garden Channel, which I refer to as "the girl channel." When the Oscars and Emmys roll around, Karen has seen none of the nominated offerings. I may have seen one or two, as I now go to the movies about twice a year, alone. The good husband, I have accompanied Karen to five productions of *Mama Mia.*

Like the angels, Karen has an affinity with animals.

Countless times we have come out of a grocery store in our rural county to find a dog in the bed of a pick-up-truck, anxiously awaiting his master's return. I will say something cheerful to the dog and may even try to pet it, but get no real reaction. But when Karen starts talking to the dog, he/she goes crazy with excitement, his/her tail banging rhythmically against the side if the truck and when Karen pets the dog, he/she collapses into a paroxysm of happiness.

Karen's Maui timeshare in Kihei is a second-floor unit. Moments after she returns each July, animals appear. The black and white cat from downstairs appears and meows loudly at the front screen door, remembering that Karen once provided some tuna fish. Birds start to appear, remembering that Karen will put out snacks. A dove appears on the rail of the lanai most mornings. Chickens from across the road start coming over, as they remember that Karen puts out seeds for them on the lawn beneath the lanai. At night Karen turns on the outside light on the lanai wall to attract bugs so the Geckos can feed more easily. Once we were walking at dusk on a narrow asphalt walkway above Karen's favorite Kihei beach, Kameole One, when we came upon a pair of ducks, walking parallel upon the grass. They let Karen, who was in the lead, pass. As I walked by, the drake hissed and charged at me. It was not easy getting away unscathed. On another occasion, Karen and I were walking on the ocean side grounds of a Kihei resort, when a nearby duck started following Karen. If I tried to talk to it, it retreated, then returned to Karen.

In the early seventies, Sam Pryor, former executive at Pan American Airlines, Republican Party luminary, friend to the captains of industry and consort to presidents and kings, had retired to an idyllic 30-acre estate, east of Hana, on the island of Maui, overlooking the Pacific. Sam Pryor was a close friend of Charles Lindberg and his wife, Anne Morrow Lindberg, so he sold them 5 adjacent acres where the Lindberghs built a lovely home, also facing the sea.

Sam Pryor developed a fascination with gibbons and had many as pets, who lived with him. The gibbons traveled everywhere with Sam Pryor, even on plane flights back to the mainland. Both Sam Pryor and Charles Lindberg contributed funds to restore the nearby missionary church at Kipahula, originally built in1854. Eventually, both men signed a joint letter to the authorities asking to be buried on the church grounds. Their requests were granted. Today you can visit the church and cemetery, overlooking the Pacific, and see the graves of Charles Lindberg and Sam Pryor. And in a line running away from Sam Pryor's grave, towards the sea and Lindberg's grave are the small headstones of the gibbons: Kippy, Ganza, Hula, Lani, Keiki, Little Boy, and Georgia.[4]

In about 1973, Karen and her husband, Bob, were visiting Maui, along with their close friends, Gary and Sherri: Dove. Gary's father, a veterinarian, lived on Maui and knew Sam Pryor. One day, Karen and Bob, Gary and Sherri, took a delivery of medicine needed for one of the gibbons out to Mr. Pryor's oceanfront estate just north of Hana. After passing through security at the main gate, they drove down to the main house and were greeted by several gibbons and a gracious Mr. Pryor, who proceeded to give the young couples a walking tour of the immediate grounds.

---

[4]   Sam Pryor, *The Autobiography of Sam Pryor*, Vantage Press, 1982. (Dear Reader, please do not leave this life until you have read Anne Morrow Lindberg's lyrical works: *Listen The Wind*; *Gift FromThe Sea* and *North To The Orient).

One of the gibbons, brown in color and about three feet tall, reached up and took Karen by the hand. As the walking tour continued, the gibbon left Karen, scampered up a mango tree, twisted off a mango, scampered down and handed it to Karen. He then resumed his hand-in-hand walk with Karen. After the walk concluded, conversation continued on the shaded lanai of the main house. The gibbon that had befriended Karen kept at her side, until she had to leave.

Like the angels, Karen appreciates gifts. When Karen is given a gift, no matter how small or seemingly insignificant, she gushes about how beautiful and precious it is to her, and she means every word. I have seen an angel pluck from the playground a sprig of clover, run excitedly over to Karen and lift that little gift up to her. You would have thought it was the Hope Diamond, the way she rejoices and praises the gift and the giver. It is lovely to observe an angel, or anyone, giving a gift to Karen, just to see her reaction, and how she fusses over the gift and the giver. That helps to explain why, at Christmas, Valentines Day, and on the last day of the school year, Karen needed several trips with a wagon to cart off the presents she had lovingly received.

Like the angels, Karen enjoys giving gifts. Karen spends most of her free time shopping for, buying, wrapping, storing, transporting, and dispensing: gifts. Throughout the year, our downstairs bedroom overflows with packages momentarily pausing in their journey on the gift pipeline. At various times throughout the school year, Karen gives gifts to: parents who helped in the classroom; her morning teaching aid; Irene

Gonzalez; the cafeteria ladies; the aides who accompanied the disabled students into Karen's classroom; the office secretaries; the Spanish-speaking ladies who assist in the cafeteria and on the kindergarten playground; the librarian; the computer technician; the maintenance staff, both daytime and nighttime; the part-time school nurse; other teachers; friends; relatives; and the angels.

Like the angels, Karen brings sunshine into the lives of others. Since she arrived at Grover Beach, Karen voluntarily picked up and held the mantle of the campus "Sunshine Person." Whenever a teacher or member of the staff became ill, Karen selected and purchased a get-well card, collected group signatures on the card, and along with a small gift, delivered both to the missing person. Whenever a member of the faculty or staff had a birthday, Karen would get a card, collect group signatures, buy and deliver a cake, get candles, get a tablecloth, decorate the teacher's room, and gather everybody together to sing "happy birthday" to the celebrant. Whenever a member of the faculty or staff endured the death of a loved one, Karen got an appropriate card, secured the relevant signatures, and delivered it to the intended. Often food was cooked and taken over to the home of the bereaved. When a child or significant other of a faculty or staff member accomplished something, Karen got an appropriate card, collected signatures, and delivered the card. When the teacher's room needed to be prepared for a special event, Karen provided some of the food, the tablecloth, the centerpiece, the napkins, the utensils, the wall decorations, the cups, and the drinks. She then set the whole thing up. (I have been with her on some of these early morning missions. It's a lot of work). Karen was constantly baking some goodie to take to school on one of the above-described missions.

Like the angels, Karen is moved by music. It could be said that music is her mantra. She is always humming a tune, especially when occupied by a task. Her clear soprano voice accompanies songs on the radio and the choir in church. Not surprising, given that her maternal grandmother played piano and organ by ear with such alacrity, that she was hired, at the tender age to 14, to play piano accompaniment to the silent screen movies shown at theatres in downtown Cleveland. Karen's mother, Dolores, also inherited the music gene, and also initially played piano and organ by ear, though Dolores eventually learned to read music.

Like the angels, Karen always ties her laced shoes with double knots.

Karen shares with the angels one physical aspect. She has the same wrist size. He wrists are so small she cannot wear bracelets.

I came to learn the love and respect Karen daily gave and received at school, and in the community.

A typical day would include: helping a 5th grade girl in the morning, before school started; delivering a gift to a fellow teacher; setting up a birthday party in the teachers' room; getting hugs from the angels; meeting and hugging the mother of a former student who stopped to tell her how much she was appreciated and missed; hugging a former student who stopped by to tell her she had been his favorite teacher; hearing praise from a visiting aide for her masterful teaching methods; hearing from the librarian that her class is the best behaved in the school; hearing praise from a visiting teacher who had just presented a program to her class, about how alert, inquisitive and well-behaved her class had been; and meeting with the parents of a disabled child who has been mainstreamed into Karen's class and to rejoice in the angel's progress.

One morning I was sitting on the desk at the green center, when her superb principal, Juan Olivarria, came into Karen's classroom with a visiting educational dignitary in tow. Juan leaned down to me and said: "Karen is so good, she makes it look easy."

Karen will hear on an almost daily basis from teachers and others who have observed her, or worked with her, in her classroom: "You are the best teacher I have ever seen. It is a privilege to work with you." Later in the day, when Karen shops for gifts, classroom supplies, or groceries, she will invariably happily reunite with former students, now grown and working at the store where she is shopping. Not long after we married, in the interest of time, Karen had to stop shopping for groceries at the large Von's store in Grover Beach. She was happily meeting current and former students, and their parents, on every aisle. She could not get out of the store without spending and extra hour, socializing.

Karen happily gave her professional life to the parents and children at Grover Beach Elementary, the toughest place to teach in the entire school district. She could have gone to other schools, where there was less poverty, where the children were more advantaged, where there was less crime and less drug abuse. But she considered her work in Room1 a calling. She loved the challenge and the angels, and their parents.

Karen spent her entire first three paychecks to add supplies to her kindergarten at Grover Beach. Over the next 36 years, Karen spent at least $1,000 annually to further supply Room 1. That is why the angels in Room 1 had access to 1,500 books; 500 toys; a custom-made doll house; custom-made play kitchen; thousands of blocks, tinker toys, and Legos; scores of puzzles; books on tape; colored pencils/crayons/chalk, etc., etc . . . . Karen removed 150 boxes of privately purchased items upon retirement, while leaving most of her supplies for Vickie Velázquez, a friend and colleague, who took over Room 1.

Now in retirement Karen volunteers every Tuesday in kindergarten at Grover Beach, and gives away about 100 books per month for the angels to take home and keep. To encourage the angels to write their names and to provide pride of ownership, inside the cover of each book, Karen had a self-inking stamp made to stamp the phrase: "This book belongs to_____."

To this day Karen misses Room 1, her profession, and above all, the angels.

I miss then too. When I go back with Karen to Grover Beach Elementary and walk into a kindergarten, happiness envelopes me, because I am again among the angels.

I'm So Special...

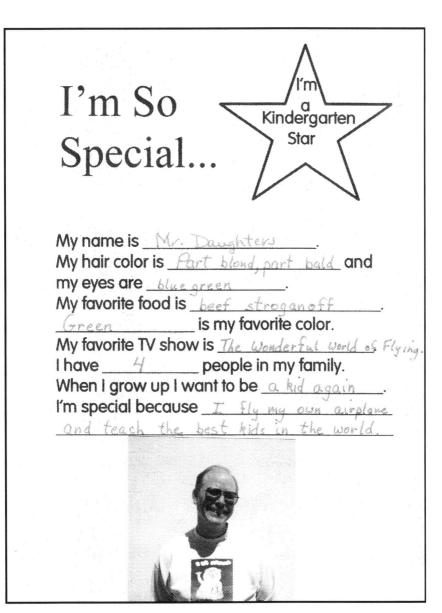

I'm
a
Kindergarten
Star

My name is _Mr. Daughters_.
My hair color is _Part blond, part bald_ and
my eyes are _blue green_.
My favorite food is _beef stroganoff_.
Green is my favorite color.
My favorite TV show is _The Wonderful World of Flying._
I have _4_ people in my family.
When I grow up I want to be _a kid again_.
I'm special because _I fly my own airplane_
and teach the best kids in the world.

Carl-A Kindergarten Star

Carl

"Daughters and Sons."

So read the sign that Carl Daughters' father, an Episcopalian minister, painted and placed at the gate to his northern California home, which he inhabited with his wife and four sons, imbued with his lively sense of humor, which Carl inherited.

When Carl and his brothers were in their teens, partly to keep them busy and partly to impart a set of lifelong skills, Carl's father purchased a vacant lot and told the boys to build a house upon it, which they did. In the process the boys developed a smattering of important skills in: planning, drafting, surveying, measuring, cement masonry, framing, drywall installation, electrical wiring, plumbing, carpentry, roofing, painting, budgeting, and compliance with the building codes.

Carl worked his way through college as a handyman and sometime janitor, earning a degree in industrial engineering at California Polytechnic State University at San Luis Obispo.

Upon graduation, drawn to children, Carl initially worked at a pre-school, but soon realized he would starve unless he got a teaching credential, which he did, in elementary education. The credential allowed Carl to teach in all elementary grades, which he did, including kindergarten, initially at Nipomo Elementary School and then at Grover Heights in Grover City. During those years Carl also became credentialed in Spanish.

For his initial home, Carl purchased an abandoned shell of a house in San Luis Obispo. Carl used his house-building skills to totally gut and remodel the house, successfully converting it into an attractive property. Later, Carl bought a vacant lot in Arroyo Grande and using his own skills and labor, built a new home. Still later, as an investment, he bought and renovated a duplex in Oceano. At his untimely death in a plane crash in November of 2004, Carl owned the three above-described real properties free and clear, all on the modest salary of a teacher.

In 1979, a happy confluence of events brought Carl and Karen together. The increased enrollment of Spanish-speaking children at Grover City Elementary required a Spanish speaker in Karen's kindergarten. Carl was transferred from Grover Heights to Karen's kindergarten at Grover City Elementary.

Carl and Karen met in Room 1 in the summer of 1979 to set up the classroom. From that moment a beautiful relationship developed, which inured for the benefit of the angels, as Carl and Karen taught kindergarten together in Room 1 for the next 25 consecutive years. Karen organized the classroom and Carl happily fit in. Karen set the classroom themes, around which she arrayed the matching books, bulletin boards and instructional materials, commencing with the Gingerbread Man on opening day.

The themes changed approximately nine times: August/ September: Gingerbread Man; Colors; Shapes; Bears/ Science and Zoo Phonics. October: Pumpkins; Bats; Plants; Fall Leaves. November: Pilgrims and Native Americans. December: Christmas Around The World. January: Snow. Winter: the Water Cycle. February: Friendship. March: Wind; Airplanes; Kites and Owls. April: Rabbits; Easter activities. May/June: Hawaii and the Ocean. Every day special time was spent on letters, sight words, phonics, and number recognition.

Karen immediately recognized Carl was a wonderful teacher. Just like Karen, he was patient and positive, yet always firm with boundaries, and when an angel needed correction or a timeout. Like Karen, Carl had high standards and held the angels to them. Like Karen, above all, he loved the little angels.

Carl focused on math and science. He played the guitar and spoke Spanish. After Carl took up flying, he produced a unit on airplanes every spring. Karen focused on language arts. She particularly enjoyed presenting the units on owls and on Hawaii.

Karen and Carl provided a safe, loving, positive, organized, and exciting environment, rich with experiences for the angels in that great and glorious Room 1, so large, airy, and full of natural light from the wall of windows looking north out onto the kindergarten playground.

Karen and Carl had two overlapping kindergartens, morning and afternoon. The morning class of about 35 angels arrived at 8:30 a.m. and left at noon. The afternoon class of 35 angels arrived at 11:30 a.m. and left at 3:00 p.m.

During the overlap from 11:30 a.m. till noon, when all 70 angels were present, Carl would play his guitar, leading the angels in his favorite song:

The World Is A Rainbow [5]

"The world is a rainbow, that's willed with many colors,
Yellow black and white and brown, you see them all around.
The world is a rainbow, with many kinds of people.
It takes all kinds of people to make the world go 'round.
Now you be you, and I'll be me. That's the way we were meant to be.
But the world is a mixing cup, just look what happens when you stir it up.
The world is a rainbow that's filled with many colors
And when we work together it's such a sight to see.
The world is beautiful when we are living in harmony."

---

[5] *The World Is A Rainbow*, words and music by Greg Scelsa, *We All Live Together*, Volume 2, Youngheart Music Education Service, pp. 16-17(Copyright 1978).

Because Carl had the mind of an engineer and the skills of a builder, he was early drawn to computers. He soon cobbled together, from inexpensive parts, a dozen computers, which he arrayed side by side on the low shelf at the base of the wall of windows looking out onto the kindergarten playground. He loaded the computers with basic educational software. The angels loved their time on the computers.

Around 1990, Carl's analytical mind sought another challenge and he took up flying. He earned a pilot's license, and with a small group bought an interest in an airplane. Carl then started volunteering with the 6th grade students at Grover Beach Elementary teaching an after-school class on flying, which concluded with a flight on Carl's airplane. Eventually, Carl bought a kit plane, which he assembled with the help of professional. Carl flew that plane for over ten years until the day he died in it.

Like Karen, Carl was always cheerful and positive. Carl would do anything for anybody. If someone needed help moving, Carl was there. If someone needed a computer fixed, Carl was there. Carl always answered a call for help. Carl became everybody's computer repairman. Though I have a new Apple computer, I intentionally composed and typed this book on the last PC Carl had assembled for me. (I then had a professional re-type the book, converting my WordPerfect format to that of Microsoft Word).

On a sunny afternoon in September of 1994, I first met Carl, just a few weeks before Karen and I married. Karen was in the process of moving out of her former home on Woodland Drive in Arroyo Grande. Her furniture (and mine from a condo in San Luis Obispo) had to be placed into storage, because the completion of our new house would be delayed until about a week after our September 17th wedding.

I observed a vintage white pick up truck, pulling a flatbed trailer as it backed into the driveway. Emerging from the driver side door, I saw a sandy-haired man of medium height, in a white tee shirt and khaki pants (this I later learned was Carl's constant weekend uniform), peering through rimless glasses, suspended above a continuous smile.

Carl's cheerful countenance never left him as he and Karen chatted, and then as he and I attempted to follow Karen's directions as to the loading of the furniture onto Carl's flatbed. Eventually, the loading seemed to be completed, when Karen requested a change in the alignment. As Carl and I labored to follow this new request, while we muscled a heavy piece of furniture, Carl laughingly said to Karen: "Karen, I live to make you happy." I seldom laugh out loud, but that remark struck me as hilarious. Everybody had a good laugh.

Over the next 11 years, I had many occasions to observe Carl, both professionally in the classroom and socially. I never heard him curse. I never heard him say an unkind word. He was always cheerful, always positive.

It takes a special man to forgo ego and significant income to become a grade school teacher, especially a kindergarten teacher. Carl was a special man.

Together, Karen and Carl took on the toughest cases: angels who had been physically abused, abandoned, neglected, or damaged *in utero* by a mother's drug use. Karen and Carl were especially accepting and nurturing angels with disabilities. Carl and Karen protected, nurtured, and lifted up the little angels in their care, with love, music and games, the safety of clear rules and boundaries, enriching learning materials, referrals to specialists, arranging for medical treatment, providing financial interventions, and hosts of hugs.

It was a beautiful sight to see Karen and Carl in Room 1, among the angels.

Even though it was "Mr. Daughters" and "Mrs. Woodward," and then "Mrs. Brown," it was understandable that the angels always thought Carl and Karen were married, as they were such a caring couple, truly *in loco parentis.*

When I asked Karen how the angels thought about Carl, she replied: "They adored him. Everybody did."

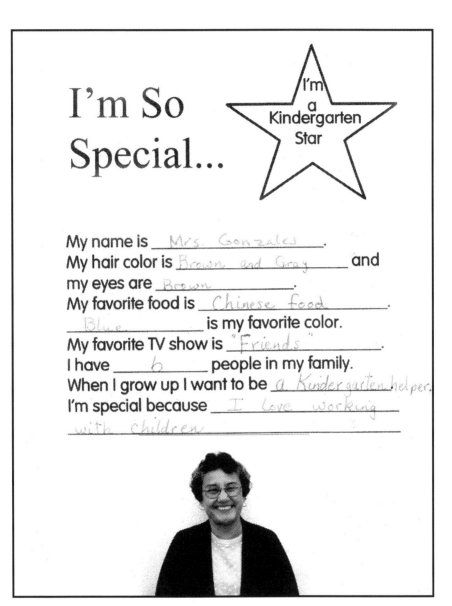

I'm So Special...

I'm a Kindergarten Star

My name is _Mrs. Gonzales_.
My hair color is _Brown and Gray_ and
my eyes are _Brown_.
My favorite food is _Chinese food_.
Blue is my favorite color.
My favorite TV show is _"Friends"_.
I have _6_ people in my family.
When I grow up I want to be _a Kindergarten helper._
I'm special because _I love working_
with children

Irene-A Kindergarten Star

Irene

Saint Theresa said that sanctity could be found among the pots and pans. That is where Irene Gonzalez earned hers. As a stay-at-home wife and mother, Irene provided a loving home for her husband, Robert, and their four children. After the children left home, Irene's home became a second home for her four grandchildren, and now two great-grandchildren.

In 1977, Irene's youngest child was in full-time grade school. Since Irene lived literally around the corner from the kindergarten playground at Grover City Elementary School, and had never driven a car, it was logical for her to apply for a job as a reading aide at Grover City Elementary. She was immediately hired. Her fluency in Spanish was a much-needed asset, due to an influx of Spanish-speaking families into the school population.

In 1987, Irene commenced working in Room 1, helping Karen and Carl with the angels. Irene learned the workings of the Hawaii English Project, which was the mainstay of the reading program in Room 1. Karen, Carl, and Irene were a beautiful team until Irene retired in November of 2002.

In November of 2004, after Carl's memorial service at the Clark Center, Irene went to Karen as she was preparing to leave the building. Irene embraced Karen and told her: "Karen, I'll be with you till you retire. I'll start tomorrow." True to her word, Irene daily volunteered in Room 1 for the

next six and one-half years, through Friday, June 10, 2011,
Karen's final day.

At the close of Carl's memorial service at the Clark
Center, the assembled were invited to gather in the cafeteria
of Grover Beach Elementary School. That is where I met
Irene. Karen introduced me to her. Though we spent a lot
of time together after I attended kindergarten from 2008 till
Karen's retirement in 2011, Irene always referred to me as
"Mr. Brown", even though I addressed her as "Irene." I found
Irene's formality to be charming.

If the devil looks for idle hands, he had no truck with
Irene. A diminutive dynamo, standing a little above five feet,
Irene was constantly in motion. I have this continuing visual
memory of Irene, bending slightly at the waist, carrying a
sheaf of papers, walking at double-time from Room 1 to her
home around the corner, or between the office and Room
1, or from the south door in Room 1 to the long counter
behind the cubbies, where she furiously collected, sorted,
and prepared documents for the centers and created all the
costumes and materials for special projects, to be used at
the centers in the following days.

Every week, at the Red center table and at the Yellow
center table, Monday through Thursday, the angels
worked on coloring, cutting and pasting tasks, as well as
handwriting, shapes and colors, matched to the theme of the
week. Each table had laminated patterns showing exactly
how the completed task should look. Karen selected the

tasks, and Irene would take the tasks home to complete and prepare the templates.

Robert, Irene's husband, retired in 1993 after a long career as a sanitation worker. Robert suffered some health problems caused by years of physically difficult work. In his day he and his cohorts hoisted the heavy trashcans onto their shoulders to empty them into the truck. Today, automatic forklifts do that same work and nobody leaves the truck. Happily, Robert has the skills of an artist. He colors the templates so beautifully, that they become works of art.

Irene and Karen have been together for so long, they finish each other's sentences.

Karen: "I think we should use the . . ."
Irene: "Peter Rabbit pattern for the . . ."
Karen: ". . . red center, but I was thinking of . . ."
Irene: ". . . using the small yellow bunny rabbit for the . . ."
Karen: ". . . yellow center, because we have . . ."
Irene: ". . . just a half day on Thursday."
Karen: "Right."

Irene shared Karen's high standards. By 9:30 a.m. on Mondays through Thursdays, the angels have each completed two centers. After snack and recess, from 10:00 to 10:30 a.m., the angels paired off and worked on: the Hawaii Language Project's eighteen levels of flip charts; letters; numbers; shapes and colors. After December, many would be reading basic books.

When an angel thought that he/she had accomplished the day's task, they had been instructed by Karen to raise a hand. Karen then moved about the room to the raised hands to test the angels. If they passed, they would get an award later that day. It was a mark of great accomplishment to receive an award. They were truly earned.

Irene assisted Karen in the testing. If an angel could not quite pass the test, no award was given. Neither Irene nor Karen ever gave an angel a pass. They had to earn the award.

Irene would always tutor angels who needed extra help. If it took 50 attempts over as many days for angel to pass a test on shapes, or colors, or letters, so be it. You could tell how much Irene cared for the angels. Her bright smile was often accompanied by a hug when an angel, who has struggled, finally passed a test, and Irene prepared the award and marked the angel's progress on the appropriate spreadsheet.

Irene was utterly dependable, totally honest and trustworthy. She had a sunny disposition and a lovely smile, which she bestowed on the angels regularly. Like Karen, she was firm with the rules and would not tolerate any questionable behavior. She was especially close to the angels for whom Spanish was their primary language.

Karen could not have survived without her, especially after the death of Carl Daughters.

Irene is an angel.

Karen's last class of angels
August 2010 to June 2011

The Angels

They are physical perfection, these little four and five-year-olds who alight in Room 1 every August to commence kindergarten.

Their complexions are so clear and without blemish as to be nearly translucent. Their eyes are so luminous; their smiles are so bright, they illuminate the classroom.

Immune to the aches and pains that afflict adults, they are as supple as yoga masters. They can easily put their legs behind their ears, while sitting on the floor. Without fatigue, they can repeatedly jump up and down, to and from, their seated "criss-cross applesauce" positions.

The heat of life burns so brightly in these handfuls of dust, they do not notice cold. They run happily onto the playground in t-shirts on cold, blustery days.

They luxuriate in rhythm, rhyme, dancing, running, and anything set to music. They live to play, to sing, and to dance.

Like tuning forks, just struck, they vibrate with energy. They are attuned to changes in the barometric pressure. When the angels get agitated, a change in the weather is coming. They are never truly still.

Their hearing is so acute; the drop of a nearby pin distracts them. Their vision is so keen, they can find and follow the path of a butterfly, fluttering a half-block away, or fixate on the path of an ant from across a room.

All those gifts and qualities, give the angels short attention spans, which are catered to in Room 1, one of the safest, most positive places on this earth.

They possess the gift to absorb the rudiments of a new language in a matter of weeks. They have remarkable mnemonic abilities.

They are quick to hug and quick to laugh. They luxuriate in the presence of the other angels. They love the smallest of gifts. They delight in the smallest of things.

They believe in the existence of the Gingerbread Man, Santa Claus, the Tooth Fairy, Leprechauns, cartoon characters and miracles.

No matter what they have been through at their young age-and the angels at Grover Beach Elementary have often been through a lot-they possess an innocence and a sweetness so compelling it almost makes you cry.

The little angels, each and every one of them, are Theophanies: visible appearances of God on earth.

Grover Beach

There is an indentation into the central California coastline, carved in the shape of a giant apostrophe, with a tail 17 miles long. At the apex of the apostrophe, the wooden Pismo Beach pier juts 1,200 feet into the ocean. Here the waves narrow and converge, creating the highest waves, attracting the most surfers. After the pier, the coastline bends southwest and a great swath of pristine beach extends for 17 miles, from Pismo State Beach, into Grover Beach, Oceano, and all the way past the Guadalupe Dunes.

At most beaches, the angle between beach and sea is acute, or relatively steep, only allowing one wave at a time to curl, break, and foam into the sand. But at the great contiguous sweep of beach from Pismo, to Grover, to Oceano, and to Guadalupe, the angle between beach and sea is so obtuse, or flat, that the shallow waves break 100 yards out, continually forming at least two, and often three, low parallel rows of advancing foam.

The distance from surf to dune is an almost flat quarter mile. That flatness has had two effects, one natural, clams, and one man-made, cars.

Pismo Beach has been for centuries as one of the great clam beds in the world. Thirty years ago, Karen could still go to the beaches at Pismo or Grover and collect a limit of fresh clams for supper. The symbol of the City of Pismo Beach is a giant clam. The north wall on the second floor of the Superior Court annex in San Luis Obispo, displays a poster-sized black and white photographs of local significance. One is of "Clam Digger Willie," a white man in overalls, rolled up at his ankles, leaning on his clam fork, next to a tarp spread flat before him on the beach, anchoring a pyramid of clams, as tall as his chest, each clam about a foot in diameter, on sale at five cents apiece. Sadly, the big clams are gone. I never see anybody with a clam fork at the beaches anymore.

The cars started coming in the early 1900s, lured, like at Daytona, by the quarter-mile-wide stretch of hard flat sand, between the dunes and the surf. The beach at Oceano has long contained the Oceano Dunes State Vehicular Recreation Area, where dune buggies and other machines assault the pristine sand, reeking havoc and increasing the populations of the local emergency rooms. I believe this is the only area in California where vehicles are allowed to drive on the beach.

Bounded on the north by the City of Pismo Beach, on the east by the City of Arroyo Grande, on the south by the City of Oceano, and on the west by the Pacific Ocean, Grover City was landlocked, until the two-lane Highway 1, traversing old portions of El Camino Real, came through town in the 1940's. It was not until the Union Pacific Railroad built a small terminal in 1996 that passenger trains first started stopping at Grover Beach.

The delightful Mediterranean climate of Grover Beach is one of the best in the world. Cooled by the Pacific Ocean, Grover Beach has arguably the freshest air in America. After traveling thousands of uninhabited miles across the Pacific Ocean, the prevailing westerly winds sweep the fresh sweet air, cool and clean, onto the shore.

Incorporated in 1950 as Grover City, the city fathers, seeking to promote additional tourism, re-named the town Grover Beach in 1992.[6]

Comprising about three square miles, the streets were laid out in a grid pattern.

The north/south streets are numbered-starting at the dunes, with Highway 1 as 1st street, and continuing east to 16th Street, then a long, uninterrupted commercial block to the boundary with Arroyo Grande at Oak Park Boulevard, a distance of 18 blocks.

The east/west streets are named. Grand Avenue runs arrow straight west from Arroyo Grande directly into Grover Beach and on to the sea. In July, the golden globe of the sun flattens as it sets into the ocean directly down Grand Avenue. If you are near the water, you may see a lone surfer inscribed within the setting sun, like the man with a plow on

---

[6] Anita Shower, *Images Of America GROVER BEACH*, pp. 36 and 105, Arcadia Publishing (2008)

the Nebraska plain in *My Antonia*.[7] "On some upland farm, a plough had been left standing in the field. The sun was sinking just behind it. Magnified across the distance by the horizontal light, it stood out against the sun, and was exactly contained within the circle of the disc; the handles, the tongue, the share-black against the molten red. There it was, heroic in size, a picture writing on the sun." [8]

Grand Avenue divides the town. The land on the south side, about eight blocks long, is flat. The land on the north side rises abruptly forming an eight-block-high hill. Because of the hill, most of the north side houses have ocean views. This more affluent area of Grover Beach provides more advantaged students to the two elementary schools that serve that area: Ocean View and Grover Heights.

Grover Beach Elementary School serves the area primarily south of Grand. It is a pocket of poverty. That area consists of a housing stock, much of which would be considered teardowns. The majority of the homes are small, probably initially built as vacation homes by residents of the sultry San Joaquin Valley. There is scarcely a single block in Grover Beach that boasts a contiguous sidewalk with curbs and gutters. Grover Beach is a poor area of San Luis Obispo County, and thus the rents are more reachable to the working poor.

---

[7]   Willa Cather, *My Antonia Scholarly Edition*, Edited by Charles Mignon, with Kari Ronning, University of Nebraska Press (1994).

[8]   ID, p. 237.

There is substantial commerce in Grover Beach. Retail establishments line both sides of Grand Avenue, from Oak Park all the way to the sea. The city of Oceano, immediately to the south, has far few commercial outlets and the housing stock is poorer. As the rents are cheaper, more Hispanic families inhabit the area. This is a source of strength for the Oceano schools, because the Hispanic families tend to be intact, with a mother at home to care for the children. The result is fewer households headed by a single female, subject to the struggles affecting that demographic.

Grover Beach Elementary

This is the opening line of Robert Frost's poem, *Once By The Pacific:* "The shattered water made a misty din."[9]

The din of the Pacific Ocean is always audible at Grover Beach Elementary, as the school grounds, a mile from the surf, occupy four square blocks, from 10th Street on the west side to 12th Street on the east side, and from Longbranch on the north past Manhattan to Seabright on the south. The entire parcel is enclosed with a continuous sidewalk and a chain-link fence.

The school buildings, all one story, cluster on the northwest one third of the campus. The remaining grounds wrap around the buildings, offering a vast expanse of grass for playing fields. At the southwest and southeast corners, chain-link backstops, three stories high, protect their attendant baseball diamonds.

The kindergarten building and playground occupy the northwest corner. The north doors of the vast kindergarten Room 1 and the smaller adjacent kindergarten Room 4, open directly onto the kindergarten playground, which abuts the corner of 10th and Longbranch Street.

---

[9] Robert Frost, *The Poetry of Robert Frost*, edited by Edward Connery Lathem, p.250, Holt Paperbacks, Henry Holt and Company (1969)

The kindergarten building, containing classrooms 1-4, like all the buildings, is stucco sided and single storied, with a roof the shape of a squashed capitol X, creating high ceilings within, and slanted roofs without, forming generous overhangs. Thus, the angels can stow their coats on hooks outside of Room 1 on the north, protected from rain. On the south, covered walkways shelter the angels from rain as they travel from their building, around the office, all the way to the cafeteria.

The original line of buildings, stretches from the center of the kindergarten building south past a small courtyard containing the school office, then continues south down a single-wide building, containing on the east side classrooms 15-17 and on the west side classrooms 18-20.

Two more wings comprise the original classroom buildings.

One wing, perpendicular to the east side of the office courtyard, contains classrooms 5-7 on the north side and classrooms 8-10 on the south side.

The other, perpendicular to the east side of classroom 15, comprises classrooms 11-14. These classrooms occupy the entire north/south width of the building and have entrance/exit doors on both north and south sides.

In later years, 15 flat-roofed modular classrooms were added. Some were added just east of the main kindergarten building, forming the California State Pre-School, with its own fenced playground tangent to Longbranch. Another group was added south of classrooms 11-14, and numbered 21-25. A final group was added south of classrooms 17/18 and numbered 26-33.

In the center of the west side of campus, off of 10th Street, a parking lot, shaped like a protractor, with the circular side lifted slightly upwards from the street to the school entrance, provides one-way access from south to north. There are 21 diagonal parking spaces facing northwest; and just uphill 13 diagonal spaces facing northeast. At the top, are two diagonal spaces and three handicapped spaces. The parking lot has a doublewide lane at the top to assist parents transporting their children. Vehicles exit the parking lot at the kindergarten playground's southern fence. The entrance to the school grounds is at the center top of the parking lot, about four feet higher than street level, tangent to the school cafeteria, protected from the elements by the continuing overhang that runs along the main buildings of the school.

Of the 500+ angels in the Grover Beach student body (not counting the 150 State Preschool children) over 70% qualify for Title One services and federally funded free, or reduced cost, breakfasts and lunches. About 25% of the student body turns over each year. The Bright Futures before and after-school child care/enrichment program, which runs from 7:00 a.m. to 6:00 p.m., is only funded for 100 children and is free to the parents. So coveted are the spaces, parents line up overnight outside the school cafeteria to ensure getting one of those 100 spots. Once enrolled, a child might stay at school 11 hours each day.[10]

In a typical class for Karen, a number of the parents will have been, or will be: incarcerated; involved with drugs, and/or alcohol abuse, and/or domestic violence; unemployed; homeless; frequently uprooted as defendants in unlawful detainer actions; engaged in serial relationships; heading single-parent households; or defendants in Juvenile Court California Welfare and Institutions Code Section 300 Dependency Petitions, where their children have been removed by Child Protective Services, for failure to protect. On average, Karen has had to call CPS several times per year to make an unfortunate report.

It is extremely rare for a parent of one of Karen's angels to have any college educational experience, a professional degree, or to own a home.

All too often, the parents are having such difficulty trying to survive, that there is little time or energy left to adequately care for their own children. Thus, many of the angels in Room 1 are cared for by relatives, especially grandparents, and occasionally by adoptive or foster parents.

The angels' parents or caregivers try mightily to love them and clothe them, and provide food and shelter for

---

[10] Interview with Grover Beach Elementary Principal, Juan Olivarria, at his office, March 8, 2012

them. But the angels in Room 1 are, for the most part, the offspring of the working poor, with few advantages. Many of the angels have never been read to. Some have no children's books in their houses. Most have never seen "Sesame Street." Too often the angels have been exposed to drugs, violence, sexual assault, homelessness, and the pervasive impact of poverty. Early in her Grover City kindergarten career, Karen made a surprise late afternoon visit on an angel's home, as he had been repeatedly absent. Upon entering the home, she was greeted by a dirt floor.

It is too facile to say that poverty is both cause and effect of childhood trauma. Adverse childhood experiences are not solely relegated to the struggling classes. From 1994 to 1998, the Kaiser H. M. O. of San Diego conducted the Adverse Childhood Experience ("ACE") study. The H.M.O. asked 17,000 of its members to relate adverse childhood experiences in ten categories, "including parental divorce, physical abuse, emotional neglect, and sexual abuse, as well as growing up with family members who suffered from mental illness, alcoholism, or drug problems." [11]

The respondents in the study were middle class, if not well off, as 69% were Caucasian, and 74% had attended college. Yet over "a quarter of the patients said they had grown up in a household in which there was an alcoholic or a drug user; about the same fraction had been beaten

---

[11] Paul Tough, *The Poverty Clinic*, p. 28, the *New Yorker* Magazine, March 21, 2011.

as children. The doctors used the data to assign patients an 'ACE score', giving them one point for each category of trauma they had experienced. Two thirds of the patients had experienced at least one category; one in six had an ACE score or 4 or higher."[12]

A tough neighborhood surrounds Grover Beach Elementary.

One spring morning, as the angels were going through their morning routine while sitting on the rug, Karen, as always, faced the angels, which gave her a great view through those tall north windows onto the playground, which abutted the corner at 10th and Longbranch. As the angel who was the weather person for that week came forward, Karen saw a scene that she would have routinely recognized if she had ever gone to a violent movie or watched a violent television show. Black and white cop cars converged on the disheveled pink house directly across from the kindergarten playground. Ninja-clad warriors, long guns at the ready, rushed the house. Within a few minutes, they brought out several men in handcuffs, stuffed them into police cars, and sped off. Karen kept the angels busy so they would not get up or look up. It is astounding that no lock down of the school was ever announced. Later Karen learned that one of those arrested was the parent of an angel in Room 4.

---

[12] ID

About a week later, another raid was conducted by law enforcement about one-half block further west on Longbranch, but this occurred after school hours.

One clear morning in 2011, I was driving west on Longbranch with a cup of hot coffee to deliver to Karen. Just a block east of school, I came upon three police cars, blocking the front, back and passenger side of a red car, with a man being handcuffed as I drove by. When I got to school moments later, I delivered Karen's coffee and related to her what I had just seen. She said just a few minutes earlier she had seen a police car speeding east down Longbranch so fast that sparks flew from beneath the car when it hit potholes across from the kindergarten playground.

Later that same year, on a Monday, Karen got to school at 6:50 a.m. As usual, she was alone on campus, though John, the day maintenance man, was probably around somewhere. When Karen got to her classroom door, she thought she noticed drops of blood on the cement. Karen assumed someone had suffered a bloody nose and continued about her day. The principal, Juan Olivarria, soon informed the staff that a gang-related knife fight had occurred the previous day. More bloodstains were found just east of the office.

There was an actual lockdown one day, because a demented person with a gun was wandering near school. Local law enforcement quickly concluded the matter. Over her 35 years in Room 1, Karen recollects the lockdowns averaged about one per year.

Just a few months ago, nearby Oceano experienced its first, fatal, drive-by gang-related shooting.

The challenges presented by the neighborhood do not detract, in any way, from the beauty of the angels, but makes their presence a poignant necessity on this earth. In Room 1, a majority of the angels have experienced a quantum of love and are deeply attached to their caregivers.

When the angels enter Karen's kindergarten every August, all too often, Room 1 is the safest, most secure place some of the angels have ever known.

Nowhere is a master teacher more needed than in Room 1. Nowhere is teaching more difficult than in Room 1. This is in part because kindergarten requires a complete change of organized activity approximately every 15 minutes, 4 hours per day, for 180 school days—2,880 educational units, but in large part because the angels have so far to go. But they get there, thanks to brilliant teaching.

Room 1

Room 1

One of the great old classrooms, Room 1 is the largest room in the school district. Most classrooms are 30'x30', but Room 1 is 30' by 53', and contains its own restrooms. The storage space for supplies is monumental.

Behind the cubbies, Room 1 offered 60 square feet of counter space and an extra sink, along with 18 large cupboards above, and 25 drawers below, the counter.

Upon inspection, those cabinets contained: 1,500 children's books; every kind and color of glue and glue sticks; pipe cleaners; white-out; glass containers of glitter; erasers; colored sticky dots; skin tone crayons; and regular crayons.

Beneath the books, running the length of the east-side counter, Karen had eight, large, blue plastic tubs, containing hundreds of indexed project materials to be used at centers for the entire year and books on tape.

The upper cupboards contained entire categories of: colored pencils; regular pencils, thumbtacks; scissors; Ticonderoga Beginners Pencils #2; Ticonderoga Laddie pencils; different sized paper clips; brass clips; silverware; cookie molds; and measuring cups.

The lower cupboards contained entire categories of: reams of colored paper; hundreds of toys; scores of games; and scores of puzzles.

Along the west counter space, Karen kept the prize box, and an open space where Irene Gonzalez daily assembled the center materials for the angels.

Between the bathrooms, Karen had a 7' two-door cabinet that contained 100 large books, some three feet tall.

Along the north wall, beneath the windows, Karen had another 60 square feet of counter space. This was taken up with: Mr. P. Mooney's two boxes of materials; her custom-made scissor holder, containing 30 pairs of colored kindergarten scissors; Tri-Task geometric shapes booklets; three vertically stacked boxes of Open Court materials; a plastic tub of glue sticks and seasonal tasks, such as colored Easter eggs, seedlings germinating in plastic cups, and topical red and yellow center materials.

Inside the front (south) door, Karen had three more storage places. On the left, was a 5' by 5' two-door brown wooden cabinet, where Karen stored her custom-made 3' by 4' envelopes, one for each month of the year; each envelope containing all the special wall art corresponding to the theme(s) of the month.

Next to that was a white wooden cabinet, with four drawers, used for math materials, and another 12 square feet of storage on top. Some of Karen's thousands of plastic shapes and Lego's-like plastic pieces were stacked next to the math center in a dozen plastic bins. These were the math manipulatives, toys and scales.

Across from those two cabinets, was a low cabinet with another eight square feet of counter space and two long cabinets below, reachable by two sliding doors. This space held additional games and puzzles.

Also, just inside the front door, Karen kept her supply of crayons in a low bookcase. Discarded milk cartons, with their tops cut off, glued into rectangles of six containers, held the crayons. There were 12 such boxes, each container holding six colors, or about 36 crayons per box.

The toys and puzzles were stored and easily available for the angels in the white wooden back-to-back bookshelves across the carpet opposite the cubbies.

Just to the west of the green language center, a vertical bookrack offered every book ever written by Dr. Seuss.

Karen had three, gray, metal, four-drawer filing cabinets. One, just inside the front (south) door, contained the previously discarded Wright Group language materials, that Karen still made use of.

In two back-to-back white wooden bookcases, Karen stored her Hawaii English Project stacks, which had been officially discarded years ago, but were rescued by Karen, and which formed the foundation of Karen's successful language program.

Room 1 was airy and bright. The front (south) wall was 18 feet high, sloping down to11 feet on the north wall. The north wall, looking out onto the playground, had 35 windows that bathed the room in natural light. Most of the windows could be opened if needed for air circulation.

Karen had to fight to keep that wall of windows. Many years ago engineers came through the school and built cabinets in all the classrooms, cutting off the light, including in adjacent Room 4. Karen successfully argued it was a safety issue, that it as a necessity she be able to see the angels on the playground to assure their safety.

I took the adjacent wide-angle photo of Room 1, while standing with my back to those 11' windows. It shows the working part of the classroom.

The angels start and end their day on the carpet to the right of the cubbies.

The early morning events took place on the carpet. The good morning song; the calendar; the weather chart; counting the number of boys and girls attending; the pledge of allegiance; counting the number of class days; sentence of the day; and sharing (show and tell).

Much of the teaching time spent from 9:00 to 9:30 a.m. and from 10-11:00 a.m., occurred at the color-coded centers: Green (language/journals twice a week with Karen); Orange (listening to books on tape); Pink (handwriting; Try Task shapes and later in the year, Journals-with Irene); Yellow (color, cut, paste and trace themed art projects, with one food project per month); Red (color, cut and paste, themed art projects) and Blue (math, twice a week-with another teacher).

During the school day, Karen displayed, on a three-foot-long oak flagpole, a flag just above and outside the north playground side of Room 1. Typical of Karen, the flag matched the season of year and the educational themes: August and September—a yellow school bus; October—an orange pumpkin; November—fall leaves; December—Santa Claus; January—a snow man; February—red and pink hearts; March—green shamrocks; April—a white Easter Bunny, carrying a basket of colored Easter eggs; May—a basket of daisies; and June—a bucket and a sand pail sitting on a beach.

Room 1 was a wonder. They don't make classrooms like that anymore. Too much space, air and light, I'd guess.

A Day In The Life Of
A Kindergartner

Karen gave this synopsis to the angels' parents at Back To School Night:

8:15 Arrive at school. Sign in for lunch count. Put backpack and lunch away, check color chart for centers, go outside and play.

8:30 Bell rings—line up at the door. Child enters and sits in his/her own special spot on the rug.

Opening—roll and lunch count
        Song: "Good Morning"

Calendar, weather, flag salute, number line, sentence of the day, and Sharing (each child has one day a week).

8:50-9:00 Share a "Big Book". Children are learning how print works—reading left to right and top to bottom, etc.

9:00-9:30 Centers
    Blue-Math Activity   Orange-Listen to a story
                                   and follow
    Green-Reading Activity   along in book
    Yellow-Cut and Paste/Food
    Red-Cut/Paste/Food   Pink-Handwriting/Try Task/
                                   Journals

9:30-9:40 Zoo—phonics
9:40-10:00 Snacks and Recess

10:00-10:30 HEP Tutoring—children are paired to work together. One is the "teacher" and the other is the "student" (individualized).

10:30-11:00 Math/story theme/journal writing
11:00-11:20 Lunch
11: 20-11:35 Playground
11:35-12:00 Language arts instruction
12:00-12:20 Toy Time
12:20-12:30 Pass out awards, collect materials; get ready to go home

Goodbye Song; Dismissal

Beginning in October, there will be small group instruction from 12:30-1:15 p.m. Individual children will be invited to stay and participate.

Every Friday: (1) Mr. Sutherland brings his third grade class to Room 1 to be paired with, and to read to, their reading "buddy", and (2) the children engage in a large art project. Every other Friday, we go to the library and to the Carl Daughters Learning Center (the computer lab).

Setting Up

I thought I'd help.

In August of 2008, I had decided I needed to experience kindergarten to better understand it, Karen, and the angels in order to write this book.

So, I went with Karen to her classroom to prepare for the new school year.

First, Karen took me to the rear of the nearby office where I discovered, racked on two metal tiers, eight thick spools of butcher paper, each three feet long, in eight different colors: canary yellow, sky blue, white, lime green, red, light pink, green, and brown. Karen selected sky blue. I then wrestled the spool off the metal tier. It must have weighed 40 pounds. I struggled to carry the bulky spool back to the classroom.

Karen said we had to line all exposed walls with the butcher paper, about 70 horizontal feet. We started on the largest wall, the front, south wall, which the angels would be facing at the beginning, middle, and end of each day.

Using my Stanley Powerlock, 25-foot retractable, metal measuring tape, I carefully measured the vertical length from top sill to bottom sill: 79 inches. I put the spool of butcher paper onto the rug, rolled out enough paper, and on hands and knees, measured 79 inches and cut. Lifting the swath of paper and holding it straight up, I lurched towards the wall. After reaching the wall, Karen and I affixed the paper to the top of the wall with staples. We then smoothed the paper and secured the bottom with staples.

It was too short! The uncovered portion tapered from left to right, exposing a thin white triangle of uncovered wall.

"The border paper will cover that," said Karen, a little surprised.

I continued the same pattern for the next sheet, and the next, and the next. My measuring was usually a tad too short, and sometimes I overcompensated and measured a little too long.

I soon said: "Here we have, collectively, two Baccalaureate degrees, your Master's degree, and my Juris Doctorate, and we can't measure 79 inches." Then it became a source of humor. "The border paper will cover that" became a mantra.

After three sweaty hours, much of it involved in the cutting out of patterns to fit the butcher paper over and around: power sockets, computer connections, permanent file cabinets, a fire extinguisher, and the sink near the dollhouse area, we finished. (Even after I had accidentally discovered how the "Powerlock" feature worked on the measuring tape, I never did manage to measure and cut a single sheet to the correct length.)

Then it was time to staple the bright yellow border paper, which was about four inches wide, flat on the bottom, scalloped on the top. After a while, I ran out.

"Don't worry, Karen, I'll measure what we need," I confidently asserted. I measured and went to the nearby school supply store and got more. We ran out again! I had measured wrongly again. So, I made another trip to the store, where I bought enough border paper to outline Lake Huron.

Finally, only a small space remained above the playhouse. Confident that I could finally be unsupervised, Karen said, "Why don't you finish that last part?"

Pleased with myself, I had just stapled the last piece of border paper into place, when I heard Karen say, "You've got it upside down."

Sure enough, I had to pull out the three-foot patch and do it right, but at least I had border paper to spare.

We quit for the day, having spent over six hours.

On the next day we cleaned the toys, all 500 of them, with antiseptic wipes. We started with the blocks, the Lincoln Logs, the tinker toys, the Legos, then all the rolling stock (trucks, cars, planes, school busses, earth-moving equipment, tractors, fire engines, ambulances), then the pirate ships, the toy structures (parking lot, farmhouse, barn, airport), the covers of 200 books, scores of kitchen utensils, pots, pans, plastic food, and regular-sized baby dolls. This took a LONG time.

At the dollhouse, I noticed myself lingering over the Barbies, all nine of them. They had to be disrobed to be cleaned. What an impossibly perfect figure, I thought, and awfully hard to undress. The custom Barbie clothing was way too tight. But with persistence, I finally got the job done. (That night we took home doll clothing and kitchen clothing to be washed in our washing machine and dried in our dryer.)

Then it was time to replace the toys. Karen sent me to the play kitchen area. I was happily placing into cupboards the play flatware, cups, saucers, and everything else.

Then over my shoulder, I heard Karen say, "Those pots and pans don't go there."

Karen then showed me where the pots and pans were to be stowed.

Then came the letters of the alphabet.

Running from the cubbies on the left to the flagpole on the right, we pinned to the wall all 26 letters of the Open

Court alphabet, each letter framed in an 18" x 7" rectangle of white plastic, each frame containing in black the capital letter and attendant small letter, with the vowels in red.

Below the row of the Open Court alphabet, we pinned all 26 squares of the Zoo-phonics small letter alphabet, each black small letter in a 6" x 6" white plastic square, with the colored animal wrapped around the particular letter, as follows: a-allie alligator; b-bubba bear; c-catina cat; d-deedee dear; e-ellie elephant; f-francy fish; g-gordo gorilla; h-honey horse; i-inny inchworm; j-jerry jellyfish; k-kayo kangaroo; l-lizzy lizard; m-missy mouse; n-nigel night owl; o-olive octopus; p-peewee penguin; q-queeny quail; r-robby rabbit; s-sammy snake; t-timothy tiger; u-umber umbrella bird; v-vincent vampire bat; w-willie weasel; x-xavier fox; y-yancy yak; and z-zeke zebra.

To count the days of the entire school year, from 1-180, between the bottom of the Zoo-phonics alphabet and the top edge of the butcher paper, Karen unrolled and affixed two parallel strips of three inch wide, blank adding machine tape, reaching from the cubbies all the way to the flagpole. The first row accommodates numbers 1-90; the second row displays numbers 91-180. Starting with the first day of school, Karen would write the number 1, then 2, and so on, until 180 is reached on the final day. (In February, there is a big 100th day party).

Next we affixed a likeness of the school mascot, Grover Gopher, to the front wall.

Then we hung the pocket calendar that the kids would reference every morning. Each day of the month had a card sitting in a plastic pocket. Each morning the calendar person would pull out from the appropriate pocket and turn over the card for that particular date and day. The month was displayed in a horizontal plastic slot at the top of the calendar and the year.

Then we set up the "Be a Good Helper" section with separate sections for the rotating jobs that the angels would have for one full week: "calendar," "flag," "line leader," "office," "lights," "balls," "weather," and "door."

Next we set out new crayons. I had never before had the pleasure of opening a brand-new, bright, mustard and green colored box of Crayola Class Pack Crayons, 17 inches across, 10 inches wide and four inches deep, holding 400 crayons. Simultaneous with the beautiful sight of eight interior rectangles, each bursting with 50 perfectly formed, brilliantly colored identical crayons, the unforgettable waxy crayon scent, remembered from my childhood, wafted from the box, reminding me again that the olfactory is the strongest human memory.

Karen used 1/2-pint milk cartons from the cafeteria as crayon boxes. Twice a year Karen directed the angels to save their milk cartons and return with them from lunch. Then she cut off the tops, repeatedly washed them, dried them, stapled and taped eight sections together into a rectangle, two across and four down, to form a single boxed supply of crayons. Into each section we put four brand-new Crayola crayons: red, blue, green, yellow, brown, black, violet, and orange.

Then we set out and sharpened new pencils. This is where I opened a large new box and therein first beheld the world's most beautiful pencils—200 brand-new versions of the classic Ticonderoga Beginners Pencil-No. 2.

A Sequoia among saplings, these pencils are over twice as thick and longer than a regular pencil, with an equally large lead and eraser. They are indestructible. But most of all, they are easy for the angels to grip. For the angels, they are the most fitting first pencils.

Next, Karen decorated the classroom with items according to the opening theme, The Gingerbread Man. (See **The Gingerbread Man**, *below*)

Then we set out the triangle-shaped paper to identify the centers: green (reading), pink (handwriting/shapes), red (cut/color/paste/food), orange (listening to a story and following along in a book), yellow (cut, color/paste/food), and blue (math).

I thought I'd help again.

I wanted to help the angels form lines on the impending first day of school, when they would first move out of the classroom and chase the Gingerbread Man around the campus, and later in their first morning, go to the cafeteria for their first lunch.

So, I went to the nearby Miner's Hardware and purchased 50 feet of a soft, fire-engine red, nylon rope, two inches thick. Knowing Karen would have 20 angels in two lines of ten each, I cut the rope into two 25-foot sections and tied a large knot every two feet. I calculated that each angel would have a knot to hang onto and have two comfortable feet of separation. I was pleased with myself.

Karen and I returned a third day to set up the tables and the toaster for the Gingerbread Man, and to dress the Barbie dolls and the regular-sized babies with their newly cleaned clothes, and sharpened about 75 colored pencils the angels would eventually be needing. I left on Karen's desk the two bright red, knotted nylon ropes for use on opening day.

Finally, we placed the little metal kindergarten chairs at the tables. These are the original chairs. They had been at the school in the beginning, since 1954. Made by the American Seating Company of Grand Rapids, Michigan, of indestructible steel, painted gray, with wooden seats and backs, they measured just 10" off the floor. They were the perfect size for the angels. Karen had to fight over the years to keep these chairs, refusing offers to get new blue plastic chairs. The new blue plastic chairs had splayed metal legs, which made them harder to push under the tables, and fewer could fit under the tables; and the seats were 14" off the floor, too high for the angels to easily access.

The Gingerbread Man

For the first 15 days of kindergarten, Karen imparted lessons using the old English folktale, "The Gingerbread Man."

In 2010, I stayed for the entire morning of the first day of school to see the classic Gingerbread Man sequence.

When the angels arrived for their first day, the room was surfeit with gingerbread men. Karen wore her custom-made Gingerbread Man dress, an A-shape, where in continuous horizontal rows of squares, brown gingerbread men romp against a deep blue background, bordered in red.

A three-foot-tall, plastic Gingerbread Man, right knee raised in a running motion, adorned the front (south) wall, facing the angels, as they sat, criss-cross applesauce, in four parallel rows, looking at the front of the classroom.

Above left, on the counter running above and the length of the cubbies, Karen had arrayed the books she would be reading to the angels over the next 15 days: *The Gingerbread Baby* (Brad Brott); *The Gingerbread Man: An Old English Folktale* (a Michael Neugebauer Book, illustrated by John A. Rowe); *The Gingerbread Boy* (Paul Galdone); *The Gingerbread Man* retold by Jim Ayleaworth, illustrated by Barbara McClintock); *The Gingerbread Man* (pictures by Karen Lee Schmidt); *The Gingerbread Man* (retold by Eric A.

Kimmel, illustrated by Meagan Lloyd); and *The Gingerbread Cowboy* (by Janet Squires, illustrated by Holly Berry).

Also displayed on the long countertop: four Gingerbread Man cookie cutters (one galvanized, one copper, one red plastic, and one clear plastic); a four-inch brown Gingerbread Man doll, a tan six-inch male Gingerbread Man doll, and a tan six-inch female Gingerbread Man doll—both with white floppy hats, each trimmed with a circular stripe of red.

On the wall above the angels' sink, next to the doll house, on the east wall, Karen had pinned six-inch plastic cutouts depicting, from left to right: the Gingerbread Man, the fox, three smiling farmers in blue overalls (one holding a hoe, one leaning on a rake and the third with a bag of corn slung over his left shoulder), a Holstein cow, a smiling little brown-haired boy, a smiling gray-haired grandmother, and a smiling gray-haired grandfather.

After taking roll, Karen explained the rules of the classroom, the inside and outside. The inside rules, according to Karen, were:

"We raise our hand to talk. That way I can hear you and others can hear what you have to say."

"We all have our own place on the rug. It is your special place. Only you can sit there. We sit crisscross-applesauce with our hands in our lap." Karen then sat down on the carpet and demonstrated.

"We are never to touch another person. We always keep our hands to ourselves."

"When the teacher is talking, you are listening."

"We do not touch any of the toys until free time. We will have free time every day after lunch."

"You may use the bathroom every time you need to go. You do not have to ask me." Karen then walked back to the bathrooms and identified the girls' bathroom and the boys' bathroom.

"Only one person at a time in the bathrooms."

"After you use the toilet, always put the paper in the toilet, flush, wash your hands and dry your hands."

Then Karen took the angels outside and gave them a tour of the playground, as she related the outside rules, which were:

"No throwing sand."

"Sit on your bottom on the swing."

"Sit on your bottom on the slide. Do not climb up the slide, only use the ladder to get to the top of the slide and then slide down."

"No climbing on top of the monkey bars."

"Sit down and hold onto the handle when you are on the teeter totter." Karen then released the angels row by row to assemble near the playground door.

Karen then got her sleigh bells from just inside the door and said, "When I ring these bells (shakes the sleigh bells), that means it is time for you to come in. You walk to the door and make a boys' line and a girls' line."

Karen then asked: "Why do you think we have all these rules at school?"

Usually one angel volunteered, "Because you said so."

"The real reason is to keep you safe and make sure no one gets hurt."

Then Karen said: "Now show me you know how to play on the playground safely," and the angels, like flushed quail, scattered in all directions for 10 minutes of gleeful play.

When Karen shook the sleigh bells, the angels did their best to form two lines and Karen ushered them back into the classroom, onto the carpet, where the angels tried to sit crisscross-applesauce.

Karen then explained that she would need helpers all year. She showed the angels that section of the front (south) wall where the phrase "BE A GOOD HELPER" was permanently displayed. She then selected helpers based on her pre-screening that Karen started the previous May at Kindergarten Roundup, selecting angels for "Calendar," "Door," "Weather," "Flag," "Line Leaders," "Lights," "Office," and "Balls." She pinned the name of each angel beneath the heading for his or her selected job. Karen then started into the daily routine.

She asked the Calendar person to come forward and turn over the day's date on the class calendar right next to Karen's chair, eventually getting the entire class to repeat: "Today is Thursday, August 18, 2010."

She asked the Weather person to come forward and move the arrows on the weather chart, depending on the current conditions, sunny or cloudy, warm or cold, windy or calm.

She asked the Flag person to step up, and following Karen's instructions, asked the class to stand, face the flag, right hand over heart. Saying, "Ready . . . begin," the angels tried to join in while Karen recited the Pledge of Allegiance.

Next Karen wrote down, on a white tape, running all the way across the classroom, below the letters of the alphabet, the number of the school days commenced, today being number one. She told the angels about the 100-day party they would have in the spring.

Then it was time for the "Gingerbread Man"!

Karen read the traditional story. A boy and his elderly grandparent make the dough, roll it, then press a cookie cutter shaped like a gingerbread man onto the rolled dough. They thus created gingerbread man is placed into the stove to cook. But the little boy cannot wait, opens the oven door, and the gingerbread man escapes, shouting, "Run, run as fast as you can. You can't catch me. I'm the gingerbread man!"

The gingerbread man successively eludes the little boy, the elderly woman, the elderly man, three farmers, and a cow, each time taunting, "Run, run as fast as you can. You can't catch me. I'm the gingerbread man!"

As Karen read the story, the angels immediately caught on to the Gingerbread Man's rhythmic, parting refrain. At each successive recitation of "Run, run as fast as you can. You can't catch me. I'm the gingerbread man," the volume grew, eventually into a final, gleeful crescendo.

In the end, the gingerbread man reaches a stream where a sly fox lures him to hop onto the fox's back for safe passage. As the water deepens, the gingerbread man follows the fox's suggestions to hop closer and closer to the fox's nose, whereupon the fox flips the gingerbread man into the air, who falls straight into the fox's open mouth to his doom.

Karen then told the angels, "Now we are going to make a gingerbread man." She rearranged the angels into a semi-circle on the rug and proceeded to replicate the gingerbread man for her rapt audience.

She went behind the cubbies and emerged with a blue, plastic, two-quart bowl filled with prepared gingerbread dough, topped with cellophane; a rolling pin; a plastic cup of white flour; a gingerbread man cookie cutter; a small plastic baggie containing raisins and a few M&Ms; and a 12"x12" clear plastic cutting board—all of which she placed onto the rug in full view of the sitting angels.

"We need to add flour to keep the dough from sticking to the board," said Karen as she opened the plastic cup of flour and pinched a mound of flour onto the cutting board, spreading it out with her right hand. The angels leaned in.

"This is the gingerbread dough I made last night at home," she said as she removed the plastic wrap from the bowl of gingerbread dough, upended the bowl, and plopped the mound of aromatic dough onto the flour-coated board. The angels leaned closer.

"Now we have to get it flat to make our gingerbread man." She kneaded the dough flat, added more flour, and using the rolling pin, rolled the dough into a flat circle. Then she took the gingerbread man cookie cutter, pressed it into the dough, and lifted the gingerbread man from the board, showing it to the angels, who were all now leaning far forward.

"Now we need his eyes, nose, mouth, and buttons." Karen placed the gingerbread man back onto the board, opened the baggie, removed seven raisins and three M&Ms. She placed one raisin for each eye, one raisin for the nose, and four raisins in an up-curved arc to form a smile of a mouth.

Then Karen said, "Now I'm going to put the gingerbread man into our oven." She rose from the rug, walked over to the low counter, next to the sink, below the north wall of windows, and placed the gingerbread man into the toaster oven, in full view of the angels.

"Now we are going to go outside to the playground," said Karen.

After reminding the angels to "walk," and placing the line leaders first, the angels were released to play. Karen went outside to govern.

With the angels thus distracted, Irene Gonzales, Karen's indispensable helper of over 20 years, removed the gingerbread man from the oven, leaving the door open. She put the gingerbread man in foil, and hid him near Karen's private sink, behind the cubbies.

After 15 minutes, Karen rang her sleigh bells, and the angels massed next to the north classroom door. Karen reminded the line leaders to be first. Karen invited the angels in, reminding them to "walk."

After the angels had reached the rug, Karen exclaimed with astonishment, "Oh, look. The gngerbread man is gone!" The angels spun around as Karen walked quickly to the toaster oven.

"Look, the door is open and he's gone!"

"He's gone!" agreed the angels.

"We had better go look for him in the classroom. Quietly, row one, get up and look for the gingerbread man . . . Now row two . . . Now row three . . . Now row four."

The angels dispersed throughout the classroom.

Karen and Irene helped look.

After an interval, Karen said, "Well, I don't think he is in here, so we had better go look for him in the cafeteria."

Thus commenced the campus tour.

Karen arranged the angels into the semblance of a line, line leaders first. She opened the south door and led the angels across the lawn, directly towards the cafeteria. This was more of a movement than a line. (See **Breaking Camp**, below)

The angels began to have sightings. "I think I saw him, Mrs. Brown," some said.

Entering the cafeteria, Karen stopped the angels, saying: "This is where we eat lunch." Seeing no gingerbread man, she led the angels straight ahead into the kitchen. The two cooks were waiting. Karen asked, "Have you seen the gingerbread man?"

The cooks replied, "I think he was here and he went that way," pointing towards the office.

Karen told the angels, "Follow me to the office. Now let's say good-bye to the cooks and blow them a kiss." Karen led the angels in saying, "Good-bye," and sweeping her right hand from her lips towards the cooks, she led the angels as they all blew a collective kiss.

Karen took the angels out of the cafeteria, turned right, and walked them under the covered walkway to the first building on the left, the office.

After the angels had squeezed into the office, Karen said: "This is the office. Here are the secretaries and the principal's office." She then asked the secretary, "Have you seen the gingerbread man?"

The secretary replied, "I think I saw him going towards the library."

Karen told the angels, "Follow me. We are going to the library. Now, best we say good-bye and blow a kiss to the secretary." The angels followed Karen's lead, said a collective "good-bye," and blew a collective kiss.

Karen grouped the angels behind her and turned left out of the office, still under the covered walkway, then turned right at the corner, still under the covered walkway, past a row of classrooms, then turned left, leaving the covered walkway, out onto the asphalt between the first row of modular buildings. The library was the first building on the right. Karen led the angels up the ramp into the library. After all had entered, Karen introduced the angels to Mrs. Adelman, the librarian.

Karen told the angels, "This is the library, full of wonderful books. We will get to come here and check out books to read, and this is Mrs. Adelman, our librarian." Karen then asked Mrs. Adelman, "Have you seen the gingerbread man?"

Mrs. Adelman replied, "I think he was here, and I saw him run towards the computer lab."

Karen told the angels, "Follow me and we will go look in the computer lab. Now let's say good-bye and blow a kiss to Mrs. Adelman."

More or less in unison, the angels said, "Good-bye, Mrs. Adelman," and with sweeping gestures, threw her a collective kiss.

Karen led the angels down the ramp past two more modular units to the last modular in the row, the computer lab. Karen led the angels up the ramp into the computer lab. The lab is 20 feet wide and 40 feet long, lined on three sides with approximately 30 desktop computers.

After the angels were inside, Karen told the angels, "This is the Carl Daughters Learning Center—the computer lab-named after Mr. Daughters, with whom I used to teach. We will get to come here often, and this is Mr. Virden, the computer technician." Karen continued: "Mr. Virden, did you see the gingerbread man?"

Mr. Virden replied, "I think he ran across the front of this building and turned the corner and went back towards the kindergarten."

Karen told the angels, "Let's say good-bye and blow a kiss to Mr. Virden." The angels, more in unison now, said good-bye and waved a collective kiss.

Karen led the angels back towards kindergarten going around the east end of the other classrooms, showing the angels the big playground used by the big kids.

"This is the playground for the big kids, but we have our own separate playground right outside our classroom door just for us, and big kids are not allowed."

As Karen reached the front of the kindergarten building, more sightings occur: "I thought I saw him!" "Yeah, me too!" "Where?"

While the angels had been on their campus tour, Irene Gonzalez had placed 20 paper plates onto the little tables, each plate containing a brown cookie in the shape of the gingerbread man.

So when Karen finally led the angels back into the classroom, she was able to exclaim, "Look, the gingerbread man got a bunch of his friends together and now we each have a gingerbread man!"

"Wow's" were heard all around as the angels went to the tables and tucked into their gingerbread man cookies.

So vivid do the angels imagine, so willing are they to believe, that sometimes, later in the day, on the first day of kindergarten, one of Karen's former students, now in first or second grade, stopped by to ask Karen if the gingerbread man was ever found.

Yes, Virginia, there is a gingerbread man.

Breaking Camp

On the first day of kindergarten in 2008, I had carefully prepared a thick, red nylon rope, knotted every two feet to help the angels walk in lines from the classroom, as they initially engaged in their excited quest to look for the gingerbread man, and later during their first trip from the classroom to the cafeteria for their first lunch.

When Karen said, "Well, I don't think he's here (in the classroom), so we had better go look for him in the cafeteria," she began to collect the angels at the south (front) door.

Karen called out the names of the newly selected "line leaders" and gradually led them to their places at the head of the slowly forming line, and behind the rubber mat inside the door.

"All right now. We are going to WALK QUIETLY to the cafeteria. Hold onto the rope. Line leaders, follow me," Karen said.

There are two routes to the cafeteria—directly across the grass, past a healthy sycamore tree, a distance of about 75 feet, or indirectly, using the sidewalk, a distance twice as long, requiring the angels to walk straight out of their classroom, along the outside of Room 3, jog a few feet left, then right, then straight ahead for about 80 feet past the office, then right, beneath the covered walkway, another 90 feet, then turn left and into the cafeteria.

Karen chose the direct route because it was faster, more melded to the short attention span of an angel. As soon as the angels hit the grass, the shape of my ropes turned into Z's, then two parallel capital S's. I tried to nudge the angels back into something like a line, but it was useless.

The angels were happily distracted by the whiff of a passing cloud, the flutter of a blackbird that landed on a low branch of the tree above them, the gusting wind, the flash of an aluminum gum wrapper left previously upon the lawn, a dark twig blowing across the grass, and the shrill excitement of just being outdoors.

As we continued throughout the day, nothing changed. My rope was a failure as the angels surged from place to place. No one ever got hurt. There was no running, but lots of hopping, skipping, sliding, and briefly walking backwards to catch a last orange glimpse of a Monarch butterfly that wafted across the path. It was a happy confusion as the angels moved in the general direction to which they were headed. They always eventually reached their destinations.

That night I said to Karen, "The angels did not so much move in a line, but surge in an intended direction. Left to themselves, they would all eventually have reached the cafeteria, but each in his own time. This is so much like the description in *The Oregon Trail* of the Sioux Indians breaking camp." Here it is:

"As their preparations were completed, each family moved off the ground. The crowd was rapidly melting away. I could see them crossing the river, and passing in quick succession along the profile of the hill on the farther side. When all were gone, I mounted and set out after them, followed by Raymond, and, as we gained the summit, the whole village came into view at once, straggling away for a mile or more over the barren plains before us. Everywhere glittered the iron points of lances. The sun never shone upon a more strange array. Here were the heavy-laden pack-horses, some wretched old woman leading them, and two or three children clinging to their backs. Here were mules or ponies covered from head to tail with gaudy trappings, and mounted by some gay young squaw, grinning bashfulness and pleasure as the Meneaska looked at her. Boys with miniature bows and arrows wandered over the plains, little naked children ran along on foot, and numberless dogs scampered among the feet of the horses. The young braves, gaudy with paint and feathers, rode in groups among the crowd, often galloping, two or three at once along the line, to try the speed of their horses. Here and there you might see a rank of sturdy pedestrians stalking along in their white buffalo robes. These were the dignitaries of the village, the old men and warriors, to whose age and experience the wandering democracy yielded a silent deference. With the rough prairie and broken hills for its background, the restless scene was striking and picturesque beyond description. Days and weeks made me familiar with it, but never impaired its effect upon my fancy . . . I have never seen, and I do not believe that the world can show a spectacle more impressive than the march of a large Indian village over the prairies."[13]

---

[13] Frances Parkman, *The Oregon Trail*, edited by E. N. Feltskog, pp. 216-218, 601, The University of Wisconsin Press (1969)

A Modest Proposal[14]

After observing for the first few days the angels' feeble attempts to form lines, I was sitting at the dining room table, just off the kitchen where Karen was preparing dinner, when a modest proposal came to me.

"Karen, remember Jonathan Swift? I've got it! Herding dogs! Australian Shepherds!"

Karen stared at me.

"I wonder how many we would need? One may not be enough. Two could keep each other company."

Karen continued to stare at me.

---

[14] Jonathan Swift, *A Modest Proposal For Preventing The Children Of The Poor People In Ireland From Being A Burdon To Their Parents Or Country, And For Making Them Beneficial To The Public*, The Norton Anthology Of English Literature, Third Edition, Vol. 1, p. 2094-2101, W.W. Norton & Company, Inc. (1974). This was the most notorious satire in the English language, written in 1729 by Swift, an Irish patriot and brilliant satirist. His allegedly serious proposal was that all Irish babies be sold, at the age of one, as food to be eaten by the wealthy English, thus alleviating Irish childhood poverty, ridding the Irish street of child beggars, and providing a source of income to their poor Irish parents. The piece was really an indirect, but searing attack on the rapacious English for their cruel treatment of the Irish, that had driven so many into abject poverty.

"Where would we keep them during the day? If we kept them in Room 1, they could sit at the foot of your chair. We could station them outside, beneath the roof overhang on the playground side, beneath the hooks where the kids hang their coats."

Karen continued to stare.

"Think how effective they would be, nipping at the kids' heels to keep them in line. And they would be especially good during recess, to keep kids from chasing each other and the dogs would love it."

Karen continued to stare.

"Well, what do you think?" I finally asked.

"That's not even funny," said Karen.

Thus my modest proposal fell flat on the dining room floor, where it remained until now.

The Gingerbread Man Isn't Real?

The resource teacher was sitting in class with half a dozen third-grade boys. She was reading to them from the book, *Little House on the Prairie*. In the chapter at hand, the characters were baking. One of the spices mentioned as an ingredient was ginger. At that point, several of the boys said they did not know what ginger was. One of the boys remembered that on the first day of kindergarten, they had chased the gingerbread man around school.

Curious, the resource teacher then asked the boys, "Now, did any of you think that the gingerbread man was real?"

They all nodded their heads in the affirmative, saying, "Oh yes, we thought he was real."

Then one of the little boys asked, incredulous, "You mean he isn't?"

Jellybeans And The Gingerbread Man

Atop the cubbies, close to the front wall, a two-quart clear plastic jar with a bright red screw top houses hundreds of jellybeans in a dozen different colors, each color a different flavor.

The jellybeans represent sought-after prizes in the class, as they are rarely awarded, and only for the most laudatory behavior or achievement.

The angels would commit treason for a jellybean.

On Friday last week, as Karen and her angels were out of the classroom visiting the library, one of the teachers of the disabled angels in the special day kindergarten class chanced upon one of her charges who, while unattended, had creatively used the cubbies as footholds to climb up and get the jellybean jar. When the teacher came upon her charge, she ran out of the classroom, leaving the jellybean jar open on the carpet, somewhat lighter than before.

Just then Karen and her angels returned to the classroom. As Karen and the angels rounded the corner to take their familiar places on the rug, they saw the opened jellybean jar, standing upright in the middle of the carpet, the red lid cast carelessly nearby.

"Oh, my, who could have been in our jellybeans?" Karen asked the assembled.

A boy angel responded with his own question, "Mrs. Brown, do you think the gingerbread man did it?"

My Favorite Book

Every Friday morning, starting in September, Karen asked Curt Sutherland, a sweet and gentle man, to bring his third graders, each carrying a book, over to kindergarten where Karen and Curt paired each angel with a third-grade buddy. The angels maintain their same buddies throughout the year. The buddies then spend 15 minutes reading to their angels. Immediate bonds are formed. These lovely sessions end with hugs all around.

On their initial visit, one of the third-grade boys saw displayed above the cubbies a copy of the book *Brown Bear, Brown Bear, What Do You See?* written by Bill Martin, Jr., and colorfully illustrated by Eric Carle, initially published in 1967 by Henry Holt and Company. Karen always used the book early in the school year to teach the angels colors and a love of language, through the beauty of rhythm and rhyme. The angels so loved the book, and Karen read it to them so often, that the angels soon were able to chant it.

The third-grade boy, one of Karen's former students, said to Karen, "You know, Mrs. Brown, that's still my favorite book!"

Here are the words:

"Brown bear, brown bear, what do you see? I see a red bird look at me.

Red bird, red bird, what do you see? I see a yellow
duck looking at me.
Yellow duck, yellow duck, what do you see? I see a
green frog looking at me.
Green frog, green frog, what do you see? I see a blue
horse looking at me.
Blue horse, blue horse, what do you see? I see a
black sheep looking at me.
Black sheep, black sheep, what do you see? I see a
goldfish looking at me.
Goldfish, goldfish, what do you see? I see a teacher
looking at me.
Teacher, teacher, what do you see? I see beautiful
children looking at me.
Children, children, what do you see? . . ."[15]

(At this point, the angels repeat the names of all the
animals and colors).

---

[15] Bill Martin, pictures by Eric Carle, *Brown Bear, Brown Bear, What Do You See?*, Henry Holt and Company (1967).

"Where Is Thumbkin?"

I first heard this lovely song when I saw and heard Karen employ it on the first day of school in August of 2008.

It was time for the angels to go onto the playground for the first time. They had anxiously formed a double line at the north door, when Karen realized that another teacher was tardy in vacating the playground so that Karen's class could have their turn. Karen had to distract the angels for a few minutes. As Karen burst into *Where is Thumbkin*, all eyes turned to her. Most of the angels followed all the finger movements with Karen through all six verses. I was transfixed at the work of a master teacher.

Sung to the tune of *Frere Jacques*, this preschool song helps develop finger strength so the angels can engage in small motor movements like holding and using a crayon, a pencil, and a pair of scissors.

Where is Thumbkin?
(Karen holds both hands behind her back with fists closed and thumbs extended.)

Where is Thumbkin?
(Same)

Here I am.
(Karen takes her right hand out from behind her back, holding it in front of her chest, fist closed, and thumb up.)

Here I am.
(Karen brings left hand out from behind her back, holding it in front of her chest, level with her right hand, fist closed, and thumb up.)

How are you today, sir?
(Right thumb, gesturing towards the left thumb, moves up and then down with each syllable)

Very well, I thank you.
(Left thumb, gesturing in response to the right thumb, moves up and then down with each syllable)

Run away.
(Right hand is returned to behind the back.)

Run away.
(Left hand is returned to behind the back.)

The next four verses repeat the same sequence of hand gestures using the four remaining fingers—"pointer"(index finger), "tallman"(middle finger), "ringman"(fourth finger), and pinkie (little finger). Where are all the men? Here they are (hand). How are you today, sirs? Very well, we thank you. Run away. Run away. etc., etc.

Shake, Rattle And Roll

On the first day of kindergarten, 2009, a photographer from the local paper was present in the room, snapping pictures. The angels were arrayed on the rug in four parallel rows looking up at Karen.

Karen commenced to tell the angels about the bathroom(s) and the rules therein.

"We have our own bathrooms. Look behind you. We have a girls' bathroom and a boys' bathroom," said Karen.

The angels looked back over their left shoulders to the northeast corner of the classroom.

"Anytime any of you want to use the bathrooms, just go. You do not have to ask me. Okay?" The angels nodded affirmatively. (Although for the next six months, they always asked to go before they went.)

Karen commenced to impart the all-important, life-long rules of bathroom usage: use the potty, flush, wash hands.

Karen: "Now after you used the potty, what do you do next?"

An angel raised his hand and was called upon: "Wash your hands."

Karen: "Yes, that's correct. But what do you do before
        that?"

Another angel raised her hand and was called upon: "Dry
your hands."

Karen: "Yes, that's correct. But what else?"

Little Joey, just four years old, blond, and bursting with
energy, sitting near the photographer, started waving his
hand.

Karen called upon another angel. "Wash and dry your
hands," said the angel.

"Yes, that's right, but before that, we have to **FLUSH**,
right?"

The angels, enlightened, collectively answered,
"Yesssss."

Karen said, "So we use the potty, flush, then wash and
dry our hands. Right?"

The angels, collectively: "Yesssss."

Little Joey, now standing, frantically waving his hand,
yelled, "Mrs. Brown, Mrs. Brown, you forgot something!"

My attention piqued, I commenced to wonder what Karen could possibly have forgotten.

Karen: "Yes, Joey?"

"You gotta shake it!" yelled Joey, proudly.

The photographer lowered his camera, and over his lens gave a wide-eyed glance to me, then to Karen, and then hid behind his lens, smiling. Karen and I exchanged a quick glance. What a priceless moment!

"Thank you, Joey," said Karen.

Joey sat down, immensely pleased to have gotten his important point across.

The angels absorbed Joey's remark without comment.

Karen quickly moved on to another topic.

Switch Blade

In her first week at Grover City Kindergarten, overwhelmed with 38 students, Karen noticed that one of her little boy angels, whom I'll call Billy, not his real name, was not clean and always hungry, asking for extra snacks. Karen asked the boy what he had eaten for breakfast. He said he had not eaten anything. (It is Karen's memory that free breakfasts were not then available at Grover City Elementary.)

Two days later, Karen noticed a knot of angels forming on the playground. She went to investigate. She approached the fast-forming circle to find Billy in the center, holding a knife. Karen asked Billy what he had. He told her it was a switchblade and promptly pushed a button on the shaft, flipping out the long blade.

Karen was stunned. She had never seen a switchblade. She politely asked Billy for the knife, saying: "I'll just keep this till the school day ends." Billy calmly turned over the knife to Karen.

When Karen had a break, she went to the office, handed the switchblade to the principal, and told him where it had come from. The principal called CPS. The CPS worker came to school and interviewed Billy. The CPS worker then privately told Karen that Billy's family was already well known to them. Both parents had been in prison. Their neglected daughter, age three, often left to wander the streets, had twice been hit by cars.

That afternoon, the mother, a very large, intimidating woman, appeared unannounced in Room 1 and accosted Karen.

The mother's first words were: "Did that little sob tell you he never gets any food at home? You know, he lies like a rug."

Eventually, Karen's innocence and kindness defused the mother's anger.

Later in the year, Billy's older brother, a second grader, came to pick up Billy. He announced to Karen that his mother had thrown him through plate glass window, nearly cutting off his arm.

For the first three weeks of school, Karen went to her wonderful principal, Phil Harden, crying, overwhelmed, saying: "'I can't do this." Each time, Phil Harden encouraged Karen to stay. "We're not going to lose you. You are a wonderful teacher."

Because of the angelic Phil Harden, Karen stayed. She still remembers what a positive principal he was. When he came into her class, he always found a dozen ways to praise the angels and Karen. A great principal saved Karen, putting her on the path towards her beautiful professional life among the angels.

Frog Pizza

Karen and Carl arranged with Domino's Pizza in Arroyo Grande, to bring the class into the store, where the angels would get to watch as their pre-ordered pepperoni pizzas were made, then eat the pizzas.

A school bus transported the angels about 12 blocks to the Elm Street side of Soto Park. Without stopping at the park, Carl and half of the angels, accompanied by several parent helpers, immediately headed north down Elm Street towards Dominos, about three blocks away.

Karen and her parent helpers watched the angels happily launch themselves onto the playground equipment: swings, slides, and merry-go-round. A large grassy area to the east separated the playground from Elm Street. A covered area just north of the playground with picnic tables and in-ground barbecues, was bordered by an area of heavy shrubbery (apparently replete with tiny green frogs).

After about an hour, Carl's group returned and took over the playground as Karen and the second half of the class, and the parent helpers, headed for Elm Street and Dominos.

Upon arriving at Dominos, the angels were herded into the gleaming kitchen area, around a stainless steel table, where two young Dominos employees were stationed. The young men then rolled out two large mounds of dough, eventually thinning them by repeatedly twirling them in the air. This was a big hit with the angels. Then the young men placed the thin slabs of dough back onto the table, ready to apply the sauce and toppings.

Using wooden spatulas, the young men had just finished applying a layer of tomato sauce to the large pizza pies when the first, tiny green frog appeared and started hopping across the gleaming table. From the pockets of little boy angels came another, then another, then another.

Pandemonium!

The adults scrambled to capture the frogs, the workers tossed the pizzas and shooed the angels out, relieved that the Health Department had not chosen that moment for a surprise inspection.

The angels walked back down Elm Street. The little boy angels didn't see the harm in a few small frogs, and did not see why the frogs caused them to miss a pizza lunch.

Dominos never called again.

Having A Baby

Maria (not her real name) was sitting with Karen on the Daughters bench looking across the sidewalk into the pentagonal sand-covered play area where the swings, slides, see-saw, jungle gym, sand play bowls, and climbing rock were located.

Like so many of her classmates, a single mother was raising Maria. Her biological father had long been in prison.

Maria asked Karen, "Mrs. Brown, do you think someday I'll have a baby?"

"After you get married, then you and your husband can decide when to have a child," answered Karen.

"Do you have to have a husband to have a baby?" Maria asked.

"It is a good idea, because caring for a child is a big job, and it helps if two parents are there to help," Karen replied.

"I don't think my mom knows about this," said Maria.

"Whisper Something To Me."

In the fourth day of school in September of 1999, Karen read to the angels a third version of *The Gingerbread Man*, where the gingerbread man encountered different characters during his escape from the kitchen than in the two previous versions.

The angels were arrayed in parallel rows on the carpet in front of Karen. Karen started reading the book for a second time. As Karen reached that point in the story where the gingerbread man was about to meet some cows, to engage the angels' ability to listen and remember, Karen said to them, "Turn to your neighbor and whisper what you think is going to happen next."

A little angel, Giovanni, who spoke mostly Spanish and little English, was sitting in front of Karen in the first row. He wasn't whispering to anybody.

So, Karen leaned down to him and said, "Honey, whisper something to me."

Giovanni whispered, "I think you're beautiful."

Incarnations Of Nicole

On the first day of Kindergarten in 2008, I met Nicole. I immediately noticed how carefully her clothing was color coordinated, how the half dozen hot pink barrettes, dangling from her cornrows, perfectly matched her hot pink shirt, set off so beautifully by her luminous black skin and her brilliant smile.

Sweet and shy, I was touched to see that she and Maddie, a platinum blond, equally sweet and shy, held hands whenever the angels left the classroom, first to try to find the gingerbread man, then onto the playground, then to lunch.

For the following days, Nicole came to class wearing barrettes in her hair that perfectly matched: powder blue shirt matched by powder blue barrettes; canary yellow shirt matched by canary yellow barrettes, and so on.

Every day I looked forward to see what Nicole would be wearing. I was never disappointed.

Eventually, I took a series of color photographs of Nicole on ten consecutive days, each displaying her matching color combo for that day.

Nicole had won the parent lottery. She lived in a loving intact family, with two supportive professional parents. I had always assumed Nicole's mother had been the source of the color coordination. Late in the school year, when I told Nicole's mother my idea to include a chapter in my book that I intended to call "Incarnations of Nicole," she surprised me by relating that it was Nicole who selected and matched her own colors and affixed the barrettes. It was all Nicole's idea.

Unfortunately, this book is done in black and white, so the photo I include of Nicole does not show the color of her matching canary yellow barrettes and blouse.

Nicole

The Father Of His Country

For months leading up to the second Tuesday in November of 2008, late-night comedians had been feasting on the advanced age, 72, of the elderly Republican presidential candidate, John McCain.

Leno and Letterman sprinkled their opening monologues with multiple jokes, McCain as the punch line, contrasting his puffy, befuddled, gray-haired presence, with that of the chiseled, youthful energy, and the eloquence of his challenger, Barak Obama.

Like she had for every presidential election for the last 34 years, Karen conducted, on the morning of Election Day, a mock election in her kindergarten.

Karen began by securing with black circular magnets upon the white board a large square poster, 2' x 2', resembling a campaign poster. The left half of the poster depicted a color photograph of the torso of Barak Obama—dark blue suit and plain red tie, smiling straight into the camera. The right half of the poster showed the torso of John McCain—dark blue suit and light blue tie, looking to his right. This photograph unfortunately posed his gray-haired eminence partly in profile, resembling the occupant on the face of our ubiquitous one-dollar bill.

First pointing at Barak Obama, Karen then asked the angels, "Does anybody know who this is?" Jade raised her hand and Karen called on her. "Jade?"

"That's Barak Obama," said Jade in a loud, confident voice.

"That's right, Jade. Good," said Karen, smiling.

Then pointing to John McCain, Karen then asked the angels, "Does anyone know who this man is?" Only one hand went up, that of Lillie, perhaps the smartest girl in the class.

Karen called on her. "Lillie?"

"George Washington," said Lillie.

At that moment, I knew McCain had lost.

The Election

On November 2, 2008, National Election Day, Karen conducted a mock election for her class, in part to get the angels acquainted with the concept of voting.

After clearing up the confusion about the identity of John McCain (that he was *not* George Washington) on the large poster, Karen told the angels that since they could not vote for president until they were 18 years old, they would vote in an election for their favorite dinosaur.

Karen then showed the angels the ballot.

It was a piece of white paper, 3' x 81/2", on which in a vertical line on the left side of the paper appeared the pictures of the following dinosaurs: Stegosaurus, Brontosaurus, Triceratops, and Tyrannosaurus Rex (T. Rex). To the right, opposite each name was an empty box.

"You will check the box next to the dinosaur you vote for," she said.

"To vote, you must show an official identification, like an automobile driver's license. Since you are too young to drive, you will go to your cubbies and get out your nametags. They will be your ID cards when you vote," said Karen.

"Next, you must go to the polling place and that's where you will show your name tag, sign in, and then vote," said Karen.

She then pointed to where I was sitting at the green center, next to the dollhouse, the designated sign-in/polling place. Karen said, "Mr. Brown is at the polling place. You are going to take your nametags with you, and go to him and sign in. Then you will get a ballot and go vote at the booths set up on the other tables. Mark your ballot with pencil, fold your ballot in half, and then come to me and deposit it into the ballot box." (Such five-step instructions needed continued reinforcement.)

Karen then gradually released the angels by rows to go to their cubbies to collect their nametags and advance upon my table.

The angels formed a line, like they usually do for such things, like a centipede, with no space between them, all scrunched together, looking impatiently over the shoulder of the angel in front of them. It took a while for the angels to sign, and most had to look at their plastic nametag to see how to write their names onto the voter roster.

After the angels signed in, my son, Will, was at the table, and he handed to each angel a ballot and a Ticonderoga Beginners Pencil #2, the best pencil in the world. He then directed the angels to the various voting booths set up on nearby tables, the red, yellow, and pink centers.

The voting booths were three sided, 8-1/2" x 11", standing cardboard sections, taped together, painted brown, with the left and right sections opened outwards, like a triptych, with the sides turned in, providing a private inner space into which the angels placed their ballots to vote.

Most of the angels had to be reminded to come back to the front of the rug where Karen waited with the ballot box. She helped the angels fold their ballots so they could be placed into the ballot box.

Twenty minutes elapsed before the 14 boys and six girls completed their balloting.

It was time to count the ballots. Karen went to the white board and vertically wrote the names of the dinosaurs as they had appeared on the ballot.

Karen then called successive angels to come forward and pull out a ballot, which was then handed to Karen for counting. (The angels glowed as their names were called to remove a ballot for the counting, and each angel got a turn.)

Karen opened the first ballot. "T. Rex," she called. A few boys cheered. Karen put a check mark next to T. Rex.

Karen opened the second ballot. "T. Rex," she called out. More boys cheered. Karen put a second mark next to T. Rex.

Karen opened the third ballot. "Brontosaurus."

A small voice from a girl angel was heard, "I voted for that," as Karen put a mark next to Brontosaurus.

Karen opened the fourth ballot. "T. Rex." Some boy angels exclaimed, "Yes!" Some fists raised in the air for punctuation. The outnumbered girls were silent.

Karen opened the fifth ballot. "T. Rex." The boys cheered.

Karen opened the sixth ballot. "Stegosaurus."

A girl angel said, "I voted for that." The boys grumbled at the delay.

Karen continued to open ballots. In the end, she opened 14 votes for T. Rex, four for Brontosaurus, and two for Stegosaurus. When the final victory for T. Rex was announced, the boys gave a loud cheer.

The boys, excited, and the girls, subdued, then formed lines for lunch.

(Four years earlier, Daffy Duck had narrowly defeated Bugs Bunny).

"Yo . . . P. Mooney"

Though long ago discarded by the school district, Karen always kept and used, early in the school year, the Peabody Language Development materials featuring the enchanting character, Mr. P. Mooney.

Karen uses P. Mooney to help the angels hear and use correct and complete sentences, develop early language skills, and introductory conversation skills.

P. Mooney is a colorful hand puppet. He has his own song, full of lovely rhythm and rhyme.

> "I'm a wonder. I'm a wee. I am known as P. Mooney.
> "I wear a hat upon my head,
> "It's bright and gay. It's blue and red," etc.

In one of her first P. Mooney lessons, Karen used P. Mooney to teach the angels how to introduce themselves.

Karen sat in her chair in front of the angels, holding on her right hand Mr. P. Mooney. Karen instructed the angels to come forward from off the rug, shake Mr. P. Mooney's right hand, and say, "Hello, Mr. P. Mooney. My name is _____."

Karen and Mr. P. Mooney

Karen first demonstrated. Shaking Mr. P. Mooney's right hand with her left, she said, "Hello, Mr. P. Mooney. My name is Mrs. Brown."

At the time below described, Karen and Carl had 33 students in each class (morning and afternoon). There was only one black angel in the morning class, a beautiful boy, Donald, whose heavily accented speech often omitted verbs. Karen determined to let him go last, so that hopefully, all 32 angels would properly model for him the correct pattern of speech for an introduction.

In succession, all 32 angels came up to P. Mooney, successfully shook hands with him, and happily said, "My name is _____." Karen praised each and every one.

Finally it was Donald's turn.

Flashing his dazzling smile, he bounded up from the third row, got right in front of P. Mooney, gave P. Mooney's right hand a sweeping high five with his own, while jubilantly exclaiming, "Yo . . . P. Mooney . . . I be Donald!"

"So Confoosed"

An angel named David arrived late for school, as the class was engaged on the grassy kindergarten playground on a field day. The angels, already divided into several groups, were happily running a relay game, scored with shrieks of excitement.

Without first coming to Karen, David immediately darted around the playground, trying to join one group, then another, then another. David couldn't find out what group he was supposed to be in, so he soon approached to Karen.

Looking up at Karen breathless and exasperated, David blurted out, "Mrs. Brown, I be so confoosed!"

Smiling, Karen helped David find his group. He joined in the communal glee.

Karen found David's pronunciation to be so indelibly charming that to this day whenever she is temporarily flustered, she will say, "I be so confoosed."

The Workbook

In June of 1999, on Tuesday in the final week of school, Karen could not conform to her usual practice of returning to the angels their completed workbooks, because events had come together in such a way that the workbooks were not sufficiently completed.

So, Karen told the angels to take their workbooks home, try to complete as much as possible, bring them back on Friday, and then she would give a prize to the angel who had completed the most work.

Just two days later, on Thursday afternoon, a boy angel arrived at class proudly waving his yellow workbook. "Look, Mrs. Brown. I got my whole workbook done!" he said.

"Oh, my goodness, honey. That's a lot to have done!" said Karen.

"I had to sit till ten o'clock at night to get it finished," the little boy said.

"Oh, my goodness! You have another day. You did not have to do all that!" exclaimed Karen.

"Nope, but I get something started, I want to finish," said the little angel proudly.

He won the prize.

"Don't Try This At Home"

During recess, a little boy angel asked Karen to come and watch him on the monkey bars. He said he wanted to show her some "tricks."

In one of the tricks, the boy angel hung upside down, not using his hands, just holding on with his legs.

As he was hanging upside down, he turned to Karen and said: "Now, Mrs. Brown, don't try this at home."

"It's A Lot Quieter Now"

A little boy angel, during a break in class, confided in Karen.

"My parents aren't going to live together anymore," he said, looking up at Karen.

"I'm terribly sorry to hear that," she said, putting her arm around his shoulder.

"They were fighting all the time," he told Karen.

"That's not good," Karen replied, squeezing the little boy to her side.

"No," the little boy agreed, looking down.

Karen said, "I'm sorry that they are not going to be together now. You know they both still love you!"

"It's okay, Mrs. Brown. It's a lot quieter now," said the boy, reassuring Karen.

Concluding the conversation, the little boy said, "My dad won't be living at home anymore. He's going to be living in his car."

Recess was called.

Karen gave the little boy a long hug.

He then went outside to try to play.

A First Thanksgiving

Sometime prior to Thanksgiving one year, a sweet little girl angel had been removed by CPS from her parents and placed into a foster home, and then into Karen's class.

The Monday after Thanksgiving the little girl angel was sitting at the reading center next to Karen and the following dialogue occurred.

"Mrs. Brown, you should see all the food we had at Thanksgiving!"

"Yes, there is usually a lot of food on the table at Thanksgiving, especially a turkey," said Karen.

"I've never had a Thanksgiving dinner before. There was so much food, I ate too much and threw up."

A Headband For The Heart

The mother of a little girl in Karen's class, whom I'll call Mary, not her real name, had been residing in prison after multiple drug-related convictions.

Before the mother, then a drug addict, had been arrested, Mary and her little sister had been living with their mother under a highway overpass. When that was discovered, a grandmother took custody of both girls.

Apparently, the mother had been a model prisoner and was recently released from prison into a halfway house. The mother was allowed to come to school to see Mary. After their brief visit, Mary returned to the classroom wearing a gift from her mother, a sky blue headband.

Mary glowed with pride. Smiling broadly, pointing to her headband, she volunteered to the class, "My mother gave me this headband!"

"That's wonderful, Mary," said Karen as she led the class in a round of applause.

Thereafter, Mary never took off her headband. She wore it every day until after a few months, her mother was finally fully released and regular (though supervised) contact resumed.

Only Two?

For Back to School Night in the fall, the angels were each making a multi-paged book about "me" for their families.

One of the pages, entitled "Your Family," required the angels to draw a picture of each of the members of their respective households.

Karen demonstrated by drawing a picture of her own household consisting of herself, her stepchildren, Will and Becky, and me. After completing her simple drawing, Karen identified for the angels the members of her "family." She pointed to each individual she had drawn, identifying herself, the resident children, Will and Becky, and me. Karen explained she had drawn Will and Becky as taller than herself, because they were teenagers and actually taller than her.

Two of Karen's angels, both from large Hispanic families, immediately asked, "Mrs. Brown, there's only two children?"

Another asked, "Are you sure only two?"

Before Karen could answer, another boy angel, also of Hispanic heritage, said, "There's six kids in my family!"

The large, intact families of Hispanic heritage have been a boon to the school. They share a common religious background and common mores, with the wife staying home to care for the children and the father working to provide for the family. The children are uniformly punctual, well groomed, and attend to their assignments. The teacher is much respected, often called *maestro*. After a large class party, it is the mothers and grandmothers of Hispanic heritage who silently clean the classroom, without being asked to do so, while too many of the Anglo mothers are self-absorbed in conversation.

Vintage Dentine

As Karen monitored the playground, a boy from the class next door, Room 4, walked up to her.

"Do you chew gum, Mrs. Brown?"

Karen said, "Sometimes, but never at school, because gum is not allowed at school."

"I like to chew gum and my mom gave me some."

He then put his soiled hand into his pocket and pulled out a piece of gum, which he handed to Karen. The wrapper, almost entirely worn off, exposed a barely recognizable piece of Dentine of unknown vintage, looking as if it had aged in the boy's pocket for a substantial period of time.

"Thank you. I'll save it and chew it at my house," said Karen, smiling.

What's In A Name?

In the 20 minutes before the angels were to leave for lunch, Karen did a language exercise.

The reading textbook, from a program called "Open Court," was the most recent textbook adoption. Under Open Court, the sounds of the letters are not even introduced until January.

Using her proven methods (a little of the officially discarded P. Mooney from the Peabody Language Development Program, a little of the officially discarded Wright Group, the officially discarded Hawaiian English Project (HEP) and Zoo-phonics for phonics), by the end of December, her angels knew the vowel and consonant sounds of the entire alphabet, sight words, and many were reading short books.

Open Court sometimes required a hand puppet, a lion, which Karen called "Leo." The book required Karen to distinguish between different consonant sounds, using abstract words, unrelated to the angels. So Karen personalized it. She used the angels' names and had them distinguish between the correct and incorrect beginning consonant sounds.

Sitting in her chair, Leo on her right hand, she would turn Leo towards her and say to him the correct name of one of the angels, "Luke." She would then turn Leo to face the angels arrayed on the carpet before her, and opening Leo's mouth, she/Leo would say, "Duke."

The angels convulsed with high-pitched laughter, especially Luke.

When the laughter had subsided, Karen would ask what letter was wrong. An angel would say "D." When asked what letter was correct, an angel would say, "L."

For "Maddie," Leo would say, "Caddie," and the angels, especially Maddie, were convulsed with laughter. When the laughter died down, an angel would state that the wrong letter was "C" and the correct letter was "M."

Karen repeated this using the name of every angel in the class.

On the February morning I witnessed this remarkable event, I had visited Karen's class on a daily basis for nearly two years. In all that time I had never heard such sustained, gleeful laughter.

So what's in a name? . . . Glee.

A Tuesday Birthday

Early in the school year I sat at the red center assisting four angels with a project that involved cutting, coloring, and pasting.

Near completion of the project, I asked the sweet boy angel sitting on my right a series of simple questions.

Me: "How old are you?"
Angel: "Five."
Me: What month is your birthday?"
Angel: "May."
Me: "What day in May is your birthday?"

Looking directly into my eyes, with a serious expression, the angel said, "Tuesday."

Living In Sin

I had been going to class daily for over a month, helping at centers, on the playground, and at tutoring. Karen had repeatedly introduced me as Mr. Brown, her husband. In case the word "husband" might be unclear, Karen would sometimes also say of me, "He is the daddy at my house."

On the playground a boy angel approached Karen.

"Mrs. Brown, are you really married to Mr. Brown?"

"Yes," Karen answered as the boy angel looked up, eyes narrowing.

Later in the day after lunch, the boy angel again approached Karen, this time in the classroom.

With furrowed brow, the boy angel asked, "Mrs. Brown, are you really married to Mr. Brown, or are you just living together?"

"We're really married," said Karen.

Unimpressed, the boy angel turned and left.

"When I Was Little"

At sharing time, a diminutive girl angel, age four, went to the front of the class with her emerald green stuffed turtle concealed in a brown paper bag. After the girl angel provided three clues, the other angels could not guess what she had to share.

After she pulled the turtle out of the brown paper bag, she said to the assembled, "When I was little, I used to carry him with me everywhere."

"Is This The Drugs?"

Each year Red Ribbon Week occurs. It is part of the larger DARE program. DARE is an acronym for "Drug Abuse Resistance Education." It is designed to give children an early awareness of the evils of drugs.

The police department sends a DARE officer to campus, who distributes to the students red bracelets upon which are written the words, "Say No to Drugs."

The entire school, over 500 students, then marches onto the vast playground on the south side of campus and with effort are arrayed within chalked lines, already marked on the playground that spells the phrase, "SAY NO TO DRUGS."

A slow-moving propeller airplane, already circling overhead, snaps an aerial photograph of the student formation spelling the phrase, "SAY NO TO DRUGS." The photo soon appears in the local newspapers, at which the students peer trying to discern themselves and their classmates.

Before leaving the classroom to form the formation for the aerial photograph, Karen explained to the angels the intended shape they were about to form on the playground, and the reason for the airplane they were about to see circling above.

Karen and the angels marched double file out to their intended place on the playground. As the angels reached their portion of the chalked outline, one of the boy angels looked up at Karen. Pointing down at the white outline, he asked, "Mrs. Brown, is this the drugs?"

Colors And Coloring

Two little girl angels, a white, blue-eyed, blonde in a red dress, and a brown-eyed, brown-skinned, girl of color in a brown dress, sat side by side at the red center commencing an assignment of drawing self-portraits to be placed into their respective journals.

From a shared supply of crayons, the blue-eyed blonde selected a yellow crayon, a blue crayon, and a red crayon, and said to her colored classmate, "I'm getting blue for my eyes and yellow for my hair, and I'm going to use red for my dress."

The colored girl thought for a moment, selected a brown crayon, and with a mixture of surprise and pride, exclaimed to her white classmate, "Look, Caleigh, I can do just about everything with just one color . . . my hair . . . my eyes . . . my skin . . . everything is brown!"

Caleigh, now for the first time comprehending the obvious, turned to her colored classmate and said, smiling, "You know that's right! You really can do that! It would be just fine."

Who's On First?

After an angel returned from an absence, Karen always asked the angel to explain the reason for the absence and where the angel had spent the absence.

Karen: "Hi, sweetie. I missed you yesterday. Where were you?"

Angel: "I don't know. Where?"

Karen: "Well, I don't know. You weren't at school."

Angel: "I wasn't?"

Karen: "No. You weren't here. Were you sick?"

Angel: "I don't know. Was I?"

Karen: "I don't know, honey. You'll have to tell me. Did you go someplace with your mom?"

Angel: "Where did we go?"

Karen: "Well, I don't know. Did you go someplace?"

Angel: "I don't know. I don't think so. No, I think I was at home."

Karen: "Well, could you have your mom send me a note tomorrow?"

Angel: "Okay."

Abbott and Costello live.

Eating Lunch At School

During the first 33 years of Karen's kindergarten at Grover Beach, when Karen taught two kindergarten classes, the angels did not eat lunch as a class at school during the normal kindergarten hours.

The morning class lasted from 8:30 a.m. to 11:30 a.m., whereupon the angels were dismissed and either went home for lunch, or entered into the aftercare program, where they could eat lunch at school. The afternoon class lasted from 11:30 a.m. to 2:30 p.m. The afternoon angels had already eaten lunch before they arrived at school

Late in a school year, Karen talked to the angels about one of the things to expect when they went on to first grade. "When you start first grade, and for the rest of your time here at Grover Beach through sixth grade, you will eat lunch in the school cafeteria."

Karen and the angels then commenced their regular, hectic, classroom day.

Near the end of the day, a boy angel whom I'll call Ben, looked up at Karen to reassure her, saying, "Now, Mrs. Brown, if you ever decide to get a job, you know you can bring your lunch and eat it here at school."

Piece Work

Part of Karen's preparation for the first parent-teacher conferences in the fall involved reading each angel's usually thin, cumulative folder to acquire as much background information as possible.

The mother of one angel was rumored to be supporting herself by prostitution. On her parent questionnaire, under the heading "Occupation," she had descriptively entered the answer, "piecework."

"Where Is The Baby?"

When a disabled student from the small Special Day Class was to be initially placed part time into a regular kindergarten classroom (educators call this "mainstreaming"), Karen was the teacher of choice.

My mother, Mary, half Irish, always told me the Irish called the disabled "the blessed."

In my tennis-playing days, I stayed regularly with a lovely family in Cincinnati, who had a Down syndrome daughter, about age 10, when I first began to stay with the family.

I immediately noticed how she brought a leveling effect to the entire family. She smiled constantly and hugged everybody. She was so open and loving, she completely disarmed everybody. She made you forget everything, empty your mind, and just smile and hug right along with her.

When my son, Will, came into my life, I wanted to strew his path with flowers. Long before it was discovered that he was a high-functioning autistic child, his nickname became "sweet boy," as he was so gentle, kind, and loving.

Later in life, Will and I would attend a monthly meeting of a group called the "Handicappables" at our local Old Mission Catholic Church. We would wheel the handicapped into church for a service and then help them to a luncheon in the parish hall that usually also involved some entertainment, and then help them onto their busses.

I am now drawn to the disabled.

In the early fall, Karen happily accepted a small Down syndrome girl into the class, who stayed half an hour, from 12:00 p.m. to 12:30 p.m., which dovetailed with "toy time" from 12:00 to 12:15 p.m.

The little girl, though five years old, was quite small in stature, and did not speak, just smiled. She always played in the area of the books and blocks and cars, the area frequented during toy time by the boy angels. Karen immediately noticed how kind and solicitous the boys were towards the newest angel, especially Anthony. They would hand her their own toys, help her select toys, give her anything she wanted, and sit near her, protectively, as she silently reveled in the place and the play.

On the first day she was absent (due to illness), Anthony, concern on his face, asked Karen, "The baby didn't come today. Where is the baby?"

Initially, Karen did not know what Anthony meant.

"Who are you looking for?" she asked.

"The baby who comes in here every day," said Anthony.

Then Karen understood. "Oh, Anthony, that little girl is actually five years old, but smaller than most. For some reason she isn't here today. It was kind of you to ask about her."

A Princess Sees A Princess

When Karen started teaching, she wore her hair down. In the fall of her third year at Grover Beach, Karen contracted head lice from a student. Thereafter, for the next 30-plus years, she wore her hair in a ponytail. That way, her hair could no longer come into contact with an angel's head when she leaned down to help.

The change in her hairstyle worked. Karen never again contracted head lice, though in virtually all subsequent years, at least one of her students had to be treated for head lice.

For her last picture day in the early Fall of 2010, Karen wore her long, blonde, curly hair down, looking drop-dead gorgeous, like the college cheerleader she once was and the angel that she is.

When Karen rang her sleigh bells at 8:30 a.m., the angels came in from the playground, collected at the north door, and started forming a line prior to entering the classroom to start the day. It was then that some of the angels noticed Karen's hair and the following comments flowed:

"Mrs. Brown, your hair is down!" and "Your hair looks different!"

Karen thanked the angels and welcomed them into the classroom.

Preparatory to taking the angels to the cafeteria where the school photographer was located, Karen returned the photo order envelopes to those students who intended to purchase individual photo packages from the photographers.

When Karen handed Alyssa her packet, Alyssa said to Karen, "You look like a princess!"

Little Alyssa is herself a princess, perhaps the most beautiful child I have ever seen. Think Halle Berry at age five—olive skin, radiant complexion, broad forehead, large brown eyes, a luminous smile, framed by jet black hair, always braided into some fetching shape, and a gentle manner. She radiated beauty.

Alyssa-a princess

Waiting For Godot[16]

At the end of each school day, Karen assembled the angels inside the front (south) door to await personal pick up by parents or identified, approved caregivers.

Usually a few angels were not picked up in a timely fashion, so Karen waited with the remaining angels about ten minutes before taking them to the office so calls could be placed to a specific parent or caregiver for pickup.

On this particular day, about seven angels remained when Karen said to Angel #1, "Who is picking you up today?"

"If my father is out of jail, he will, or else my grandfather," came the reply.

Spontaneously, Angel #2 said, "My dad was in jail."

To which Angel #3 volunteered, "My dad was in jail, too!"

Which caused Angel #4 to say, "I don't know who my dad is."

---

[16] In Samuel Beckett's seminal play, *Waiting for Godot*, two characters, Vladimir and Estragon, on a spare set, muse about the mundane and the mystical as they await, over a period of two days, the arrival of someone named Godot, who never appears. The dialogue contains so many religious, Christian allusions, that it has been surmised that Godot is a metaphor for God.

Which occasioned Angel #5 to share, "I don't have a dad."

Which required Angel #6 to say, "My mom was in jail."

Which made Angel #7 say, "My mom, she ain't in jail no more."

Salvaging a teachable moment amid the silence, Karen told Angel #7 and the assembled, "You would properly say, 'My mom isn't in jail anymore.'"

The angels exchanged these honest thoughts, without teasing, hazing, or editorial comment. As usual, they just absorbed the sad reality of it all.

Getting A Man

Sitting next to Karen at the green center, during a lull in the language lesson, a girl angel surprised Karen with this question, "Mrs. Brown, you got yourself a man?"

"Yes, I have a husband," Karen replied.

"I'm never gonna have a man. They hit you and are mean to you," offered the angel.

"Oh, no, all men are not like that. Most men are good and kind," said Karen.

Forcefully concluding the conversation, the angel averred, "No, I'm never gonna get me a man."

"Loves His Gang"

Karen noticed one of the boy angels on the playground, strutting and using hand gestures that Karen understood to be gang-inspired activity.

Karen intercepted the angel to tell him, "We never walk like a gang member or use gang hand signs at school."

To which the boy rebutted, "But my dad loves his gang."

Mrs. Brown Finds Work

Early one evening Karen went into old town Arroyo Grande to assist at a school fundraiser at Klondike's Pizza, a local landmark, housed in the basement of a two-story brick building, in old Arroyo Grande, featuring an Alaskan décor, including an enormous moose head on the wall, next to the player piano, sitting on a cement floor topped with the crunchy residue of a zillion peanut shells, which for years the patrons had been encouraged to toss onto the floor.

That night, when customers placed their orders at the first counter and mentioned Grover Beach Elementary School, a portion of the proceeds went to the school.

Karen temporarily fulfilled the roll of waitress. She retrieved orders from the kitchen, delivered food to the patrons at their tables, and bussed empty tables.

Karen met, hugged, and conversed with the mother of a current student, a girl angel. The mother, alone, was also waiting to pick up a pizza to take home to her family.

The following day, the same mother arrived to pick up her daughter. It was then that she told Karen this sweet story.

"Last night when I got home with the pizza from Klondike's, I told my daughter that I had seen Mrs. Brown waiting on tables at Klondike's."

My daughter then exclaimed, "Well . . . she finally got a job!"

Pavlov's Gulls[17]

Level with and just 50 yards off shore from the gazebo
on the cliff in Shell Beach where Karen and I were married,
a colony of seagulls, one thousand strong, thrives upon a
smooth gay rock, thrusting 100 feet above the surf. The top
of the rock resembles the size and shape of the deck of an
aircraft carrier, but with an undulation to assist with launches,
dyed white by the droppings of the gulls.

Liftoff occurs not long after dawn, forming a white,
smoke-like plume as most of the gulls head east over the
coastal hills toward the easy pickings at the Cold Canyon
Landfill, five miles inland.

After early morning at the landfill, the plume returns to the
sea where they hunt for the rest of the day in the sea and
surf, hugging the 17-mile curve of beach from the Pismo Pier
to Grover Beach, Oceano, and the Guadalupe Dunes.

About 10:00 a.m., a few of the smarter birds soar a few
seconds east from the surf to Grover Beach Elementary.
They know from experience that 60 angels will soon rush

---

[17] In 1904, the Russian scientist Ivan Pavlov received the Nobel Prize
in Physiology or Medicine for his work on conditioned reflexes.
In a series of experiments, he found that if he rang a bell when his
laboratory dogs were fed, after a while, if he merely rang the bell, the
dogs would drool, even though no food was present.

onto the kindergarten playground, spilling some of their snacks. More easy pickings.

They arrive, settle, and perch on the chain-link fence on the north, Longbranch Street side, of the playground. It gives them a better view. If the angels disturb them, they easily lift themselves onto the slanted kindergarten roof that overhangs the south side of the playground, out of reach.

When Karen shook her sleigh bells to signal an end to recess time, the birds partially unfurled their wings. The angels rushed to the back door and entered the classroom. After the children had entered the room, the gulls swooped down onto the playground and gulped the bits of snack food accidentally dropped, bits of: popcorn, chips, peanuts, pretzels, goldfish, and animal and graham, crackers.

There is a pecking order. The oldest, pure white gulls, eat first, followed by the less mature gulls still feathered with some splotches of gray, followed by the juvenile gulls with all gray feathers. Other local birds, based on size, sometimes appear after the gulls and eat in order, if at all: crows, blackbirds, sparrows, and finches. It is fun to see a sly sparrow occasionally dart in and successfully steal a crumb from a slower, bigger bird. The finches rarely get anything.

All good things come to an end. Eventually the gulls were becoming a problem, so Karen made the angels eat their snacks in the room.

An isolated older gull, pure white, still stops by to check the playground on an almost daily basis. And whenever a class birthday party occurs and cupcakes are eaten outside on the circle, word somehow spreads, and the gulls come back in a whirr of wings.

A Motorcycle Racer

Little Artie was the smallest boy angel in the class, cute as a button.

Early in the year, Karen helped the angels enter answers onto a one-page paper that contained, in the upper left-hand corner, a color photo of the angel and the answers to a series of questions, one of which was, "What do you want to do when you grow up?"

Karen was sitting, pencil in hand, at the table with Artie as she solicited his answers to write them onto his biographical page.

When Karen asked Artie what he wanted to become when he grew up, Artie looked up at Karen and with a serious expression, answered, "A motorcycle racer, after I get training wheels on it, Mrs. Brown."

A Little Too Clean

Once hand sanitizing lotion became available, Karen used it liberally and often in the classroom. The angels called the lotion "hanatizer."

Each angel's hands are squirted with hand sanitizing lotion before snacks, before leaving the classroom on the way to the cafeteria for lunch, and before any classroom activity involving food.

This was a bit much for a boy angel.

As Karen squirted his hands with the sanitizer, he said, "You really like this stuff, don't you, Mrs. Brown?"

"A Ticker"

A sweet thing happened today.

Karen had noticed that one of her little boy angels had a common problem. He could not make "s" sounds or pronounce words with "s" blends, and other letter sounds, too.

She immediately referred the matter to the speech therapist.

The speech therapist met with the little angel and confirmed Karen's thought that he needed speech therapy.

The speech therapist employs a series of rewards to encourage her clients, one of which is to give a sticker for a job well done.

Fresh from his first session with the speech teacher, smiling from ear to ear, the little angel burst into the classroom waving a bright yellow sticker, proudly proclaiming, "Look, Mrs. Brown, I got a ticker!"

"That's wonderful, _____. I'm so proud of you," said Karen.

"An E-Ward"

Karen praised the angels with awards as they successfully learned numbers, shapes, and colors, and progressed through each of the 18 steps in her year-long reading/language program, culminating in the reading of small books.

These awards were achieved during tutoring time from 10:00 a.m. to 10:30 a.m., Monday through Thursday. An angel who had mastered a particular step on the program then tutored another angel who had yet to master that step.

For example, an angel who has previously checked out on colors and received an award for the same, would then tutor another angel who needed to check out on colors. After the tutor/pupil pair felt that the pupil has mastered the colors, the tutored angel raised his/her hand so that Karen could come by the table and check to see if the student knew his/her colors. If so, Karen wrote an award certificate and made a mark on her spreadsheet and in the student's record folder.

These awards were not idly given. Many times in my first year in Karen's classroom, I would work with an angel, think that he/she had mastered the task only to have Karen come by to check and find the angel wanting. She would return the material to me, saying, "Do it again."

An example was the first reading book: "An Apple." I was to read the book to the angel, twice. He/she was to read it back to me, twice. That accomplished, I had my charge raise her hand. Karen came by to check. She asked the angel, "How many people are in this story? Who are they? Who did the apple run from first . . . second . . . third? Did anybody catch the apple?"

It was an inquisition! Memories of my first year of law school leapt to mind. Then she had the angel read the most difficult passage, and after she had successfully done it ALL CORRECTLY, then she qualified for an award.

Karen had such high standards. She did it at every turn and in every test. The angels really had to earn their awards. They had to understand what they were doing and reading. Karen maintained those high standards from the day she started teaching till the day she left. The angels had to actually LEARN. It was beautiful to see.

Karen presented the awards printed on 4" x 6" pastel-colored sheets of blue, gold, or green before the angels were released to go home. When the angels came forward to receive their awards from Karen, Karen led the applause. The angels' smiles would have lit the world. They were so justifiably proud. The first angels to be released to get ready to go home, or to get extra toy time, were those that had earned awards that day and their tutors.

When a boy angel received his first award for knowing his colors, when as his mother picked him up at the doorway to the classroom, he proudly exclaimed to her, "Look, I got an E-Ward!"

A Parking Lot Meeting

On a Saturday after Thanksgiving, Karen pulled into the parking lot of Miner's Hardware store in Arroyo Grande, intending to enter the store to purchase hooks upon which to hang her outdoor Christmas lights.

She parked on the driver's side of a white van with a commercial decal on the side indicating the name of a plumbing business. As she exited her vehicle, so did the man who had been driving the van. Karen exchanged a glance with the man and said, "Hi."

The man looked carefully at Karen, and then asked, "Were you my kindergarten teacher?"

Karen replied, "Well, I may have been. I've been a kindergarten teacher at Grover Beach Elementary for many years. What's your name?"

The man told her.

"Oh, yes, I was your teacher! You've changed since you were five years old," exclaimed Karen.

"Yes, I have," he said.

"I'm surprised you recognized me," said Karen.

"Oh, I always remembered you because you were such an important teacher to me. It was the most wonderful year I ever had at school," he said.

"Thank you. This is my last year of teaching. I'm going to have a retirement party in June at a Grover Beach Park. I'll put a notice in the newspaper. I hope you can come," said Karen.

"I'd like to come," he said.

"See you."

"See you."

"It's 15:30!"

Little angel Nico was anxious to put on his Halloween costume, because he knew that then the angels would parade around the kindergarten playground, and then around the school, then return to kindergarten for a class party, parents, and siblings invited.

At the start of class at 8:30 a.m., Karen told the angels they would be putting on their costumes to begin the festivities at 11:20 a.m.

A few minutes later, Nico excitedly told Karen, "Mrs. Brown, it's 15:30, time to put on our costumes!"

"The Biggest CD"

On the opening day of school, Karen commenced to play the song that the angels would sing every morning for the entire year, the "Good Morning" song, music and lyrics by Bill Fletcher.

From the box of album covers on top of the small credenza next to her chair, Karen removed the large album, "We All Live Together," Volume 2, containing the "Good Morning" song.

From the album cover Karen removed a black 33-1/3 rpm record.

The angels were wide eyed.

She placed the album onto the moving turntable of the old black record player that sat next to the box of records. (Karen used that old record player daily for 35 years; from the day she got there till the day she retired).

The heads of the angels in the front row moved in simultaneous semicircular motions, trying to follow the utterly unfamiliar circular movement of the turntable.

An angel spontaneously said, "That's the biggest CD I've ever seen!"

The "Sweatshort"

Just outside and to the right of the classroom door on the (north) playground side, a single row of 35 metal hooks secured beneath the classroom windows awaited the angels' backpacks and outer garments. The roof had a ten-foot overhang, protecting the area from the elements.

At recess on a cool day, Karen was standing near the backpacks when she overheard the angel Ariel tell the angel Artie to put on his "sweatshort."

The Phalanx[18]

In January of Karen's first year of teaching kindergarten at Grove City Elementary School (to encourage tourism, the city fathers changed the name from "Grover City" to "Grover Beach" in 1992), she sent home a note with a boy angel, whom I'll call Billy (not his real name), notifying his parents of the five letters of the alphabet that still eluded Billy, asking them to help drill the boy to learn them, indicating that he could get an award when he knew all his letters. By the time that note went home, just after Christmas vacation, virtually the entire class could identify all the capital and small letters of the alphabet, and recognize the sounds attributed to each letter.

On this January morning at about 8:15 a.m., Karen stood near the center island behind the rug, where her Hawaiian English Project (HEP) materials were kept, watching the angels as they entered the classroom to start a new school day.

Coming purposefully through the south door into the room, bringing his son quickly by the hand, Karen saw the father of Billy dressed in jeans and a blue work shirt,

---

[18] The impenetrable military formation known as the phalanx, evidenced by close and deep ranks of infantry shields, joined together with spears overlapping, when employed by Alexander the Great, allowed him to conquer, in the third century before Christ, nearly the entire ancient world.

frowning. As he released his son's hand, now glaring at Karen, he exploded, "It's not MY JOB to teach him. It's YOUR JOB! That's what you get paid for."

Karen saw the look of horror on Billy's face as he ran to Karen, wrapping his arms around her waist as Karen laid her left arm across the back of his shoulders.

Fearful, Karen put her right palm up to block the father's advance, saying, "It's okay, Mr. _____. Don't worry. This is not a problem."

He stopped less than six feet away from Karen, fists clenched. Karen then smelled the sour reek of alcohol from his open mouth and saw the bloodshot eyes glowering from his unshaven face. Karen kept her eyes glued on the angry father.

Karen's heart and mind raced. She could not run from the room for help and abandon the angels. Anyway, the drunken man was blocking her path to the door. She had no telephone in the room. Cell phones had not been invented. Screaming for help was a possibility, but she feared it would further inflame the drunken father and panic the angels. Until then, Karen had never experienced a drunken rage.

"You're supposed to teach the alphabet, NOT ME. It's YOUR JOB!" raged the drunken father, spittle flying from his mouth.

"That's all right, Mr. _____. I'll take care of it. No problem," managed a breathless Karen.

"Well . . . it's not MY JOB!" he yelled again, leaning unsteadily forward.

Karen continued to try to diffuse his rage. "That's fine, Mr. _____. Everything's going to be okay."

After what seemed like forever, the drunken man turned unsteadily on his heels and lurched from the room.

It was only then that Karen looked down to notice that the angels had formed a protective arc, a phalanx, around her. The boys, shoulder to shoulder, arms crossed in front, the girls, shoulder to shoulder, behind the boys.

After calming the angels, Karen ran to the principal's office and tearfully described what had just happened. Police officers soon arrived. The man was charged. A protective order was immediately issued.

A decent denouement concluded this emotional event.

The father honored the restraining order. He never caused another problem.

And angel Billy soon mastered the alphabet.

Vice Presidential Material

Three young ladies, teachers-to-be from the Cal Poly Education Department, came today to practice on the angels.

California Polytechnic State University at San Luis Obispo is often called the jewel in the crown of the 23 campuses in the California State University system. With its renowned architecture, engineering, and agricultural schools, bucolic setting, nearby pristine beaches and mountain trails, and where an equestrian can board his/her own horse on campus; over 30,000 students annually apply for about 3,000 places. An high school grade point average of 4.0 is a must.

One of the young ladies, whom I'll call "Danielle," for reasons explained below, came to the front of the class to announce that her lesson would be "The Garden."

She asked the angels if they could name any plants that grew in a garden. Hands were raised. Angels were called upon.

The first angel volunteered, "Carrots."

Danielle turned to the white board directly behind her and in black marker printed the word "Carrots."

Danielle called on a second angel, who offered, "Pumpkin."

Danielle turned to the white board and wrote the word "Pumpkin."

A third angel volunteered, "Lettuce."

Danielle turned to the white board and below the word "Pumpkin," wrote "Let . . ." and paused. She then turned away from the board and looked quizzically towards her fellow student teachers in the back of the room, one of who volunteered, ". . . tuce." Relieved, Danielle added "tuce" to form the word "lettuce."

Danielle called upon another angel, who said, "Tomatoes."

Danielle turned back to the white board and beneath the word "lettuce" confidently wrote the word "**tomatos**."

Sitting in the back of the room next to the gifted mastery tutor, Caitlyn, I leaned over and whispered to her, "Isn't there an 'e' in tomatoes?" She nodded in the affirmative.

Danielle called on the next angel who said, "Zucchini."

This was going to be trouble.

Danielle wrote **"zuc . . . ,"** paused and again turned and looked wistfully to the back of the room. No help was available from her classmates, members of the spell-check generation. Thus, Danielle completed the word, spelling it, "**zuchini**."

I whispered again to Kaitlin, "Aren't there two 'c's' in zucchini?" She agreed.

By now we were both appalled.

The angels offered two other words, "apple" and "strawberry."

The angels were then sent to their tables each with a page containing six identical pre-printed incomplete sentences: "In my garden I can grow _____." The angels were expected to fill in the blanks with vegetable names from the white board.

To further confound the angels, Danielle also incorrectly wrote "**tomatos**" and "**zuchini**" when she wrote the names of all the offered vegetables onto the other white board on the west classroom wall.

The angels dutifully wrote, *inter alia*, "**tomatos**" and "**zuchini**" onto their papers, which Danielle dutifully collected, successfully completing her lesson.

In mid-June, 1992, while campaigning for the office of Vice President of the United States, the photogenic Dan Quayle, as dashing as he was dumb, regrettably was made the judge at a middle school spelling bee in Trenton, New Jersey. After the young student correctly spelled "potato," Senator Quayle corrected the innocent speller, stating that potato was properly spelled "potatoe."

Thus, I concluded that Danielle was vice presidential material.

"What Is A Sentence?"

Mid-morning today, the three Cal Poly student teachers, all attractive young women, again descended upon the angels for a "learn by doing" exercise for teaching a kindergarten class.

The young student teacher, different from the one last week who could not spell "tomatoes," walked to the front of the room. Arrayed before her, sitting criss-cross-applesauce, were 24 angels, only three of whom could tie their own shoes.

She commenced for her 15-minute lesson, saying, "Today we are going to write a sentence."

The angels squirmed.

"What is a sentence?" she asked, waiting for an answer.

The angels squirmed. I squirmed, because the angels should never have been asked for a definition they could not possibly supply.

No hands were raised.

The student teacher moved on.

I keep in the classroom a box of my old office letterhead in case I have to note something lovely the angels have done so I won't forget, or to play impromptu games of tic-tac-toe with the angels on those few occasions when they finish a center early or during toy time, upon request.

I went to the box, pulled out a page of stationery, and using my favorite pencil, a Ticonderoga Beginners Number 2, printed the following:

Question: "What is a sentence?"

Answer: "Though it may consist of a one-word imperative exclamation, a sentence is a grouping of consecutive words, containing at minimum, a subject, a verb, and a predicate, commencing with a capital letter, ending with a period, question mark, or exclamation point, conveying a thought."

Such a simple answer.

I signed the paper with the following incomplete sentence: "W.L. Brown, Bachelor of Arts, Juris Doctorate."

What's A Copycat?

After Karen first used the word "copycat" in the classroom, she then asked the angels, "What's a copycat?"

Karen then called upon the only angel who had raised her hand to answer.

The angel correctly, though ungrammatically, answered: "It's like when one people do's what the other people do's."

Lowering Cholesterol

A Grover Beach first-grade teacher told Karen this story:

At a time when a nationwide ad campaign touted eating Cheerios as a way to lower cholesterol, the first-grade teacher had placed onto the front of her desk a large yellow box of Cheerios, intending to use some of the contents later that morning in a math lesson.

As her students entered the classroom and passed by her desk, they saw the Cheerios box, resulting in the following exchanges.:

Student #1: "What are you going to do with the Cheerios?"

Teacher: "We'll talk about that later."

Student #2: "Are we having a snack of Cheerios?"

Teacher: "We'll talk about that later."

Student #3: "Are we making an art project with the Cheerios?"

Teacher: We'll talk about that later."

Student #4: an autistic boy, remarked: "I see you're trying to lower your cholesterol."

The Cell Phone

Some days after I had provided Karen with a new cell phone, Karen placed her old, presumably inoperative, cell phone into the playhouse for the angels to enjoy.

Several days later Karen noticed one of the little girl angels using the cell phone. The little girl then walked over to Karen, handed her the cell phone, and said, "Here, somebody wants to talk to you."

Karen went along with the pretend game, so she took the cell phone, saying, "Hello, this is Mrs. Brown."

Karen then heard the distinctive click of a hang-up sound. She pulled the phone away from her ear and looked at it. Lights flashed on the phone. Surprised, Karen looked down at the waiting girl angel, exclaiming, "This is a real phone!"

"Yeah, people talk on it," sighed the girl angel, stating the blatantly obvious.

The phone remained illuminated for 15 more minutes. After the battery ran down, Karen removed the battery and returned the cell phone, now finally inoperative, to the playhouse.

A Precious Box Of Chocolates

Karen's campus published a *Grover Gopher Gazette*, where, in an article written by a student, Karen was honored as Teacher of the Month. The writer had interviewed Karen and had written that Karen liked chocolate.

On the morning of the day after the article appeared, one of Karen's little boy angels came into class holding a small box. He walked up to Karen and handed up to her the box, smiling sweetly, saying, "You're the best teacher in the whole world, and I got you a box of chocolates."

Karen beamed and in an excited voice exclaimed, "Oh, _____, thank you so much. I love chocolates," as she hugged him, humbled by the thought that she was the only teacher he had ever known.

Later that afternoon, Karen saw his mother and thanked her profusely for such a lovely gift.

His mother replied, "You deserved a lot more, but it's all we could afford."

"The Best Day Ever"

In the late spring of each year, Karen taught a unit focused on Hawaii. She ended the two-week period with the angels dancing and singing the Hukilau, followed by a class party, which Karen called a luau.

Over a two-week period, this required the making of hula skirts, tops, loincloths, leis, headbands, and various other Hawaiian paraphernalia. Karen created the costume patterns and Irene traced the patterns for the other two kindergartens. Karen then taught the lyrics and hand movements to accompany the Hukilau, with multiple rehearsals, so the angels, all 90 of them, could dance and sing the Hukilau to their parents on the kindergarten playground, which had just concluded.

For the luau, Karen had purchased all sorts of tropical fruits: mangoes, pineapples, guavas, bananas, persimmons, and figs, which she had placed at tables all over the classroom for cutting and eating.

As the fully costumed angels scattered to the tables and commenced cutting up the fruits, assisted by family and friends, Karen felt exhausted, utterly worn out.

The angels were beside themselves with excitement, trying unsuccessfully not to run from table to table, all in costume, to experience different kinds of fruit. Karen was just thinking to herself, "I don't see how I can ever do all this again!" when a girl angel came up to her, beaming with happiness to say:

"Mrs. Brown, isn't this just the best day ever?"

"Happy Valentine's Day"

On Valentine's Day, Karen saw one of her boy angels getting out of his mother's car as she dropped him off at school. He was a sweet, but extremely overweight, little boy.

Karen then noticed he was carrying a small box of Whitman chocolates. As his mother's car drove off, Karen saw the little boy open the box and stuff many pieces of chocolate into his mouth, and replace the lid. Walking slowly, but chewing vigorously, he made his way towards the classroom.

As he entered the classroom, telltale chocolate dripped from both sides of his mouth, as he handed Karen the box, mumbling: "Happy Valentine's Day."

Karen thanked him and opened the box.

It was empty.

"My Dad Has A New Home"

Karen sat at a center with five angels making personalized banners to be hung in the classroom when their parents came to the classroom for the impending Back to School Night.

Each banner needed the angel's name, date of birth, names of family members and pets in the home, and the names of favorite television programs—essentially a bio for each child.

Karen solicited the information from each angel and completed the banner while the other angels colored.

Karen got to a little boy angel. He told Karen he had a mom and a sister, but no father in the house. A girl angel sitting at the center asked, "You don't have a dad that lives in your house?"

The boy angel said, "No, my dad has a new home. It's called prison. And he gets to live there a whole long time, and they feed him, too.

The other angels at the table absorbed his answer without reaction or comment.

The little boy angel was so innocent; he had no idea that prison was a bad place.

But towards the end of the school year, the boy angel became more guarded about discussing his father and prison.

A Brilliant Smile

A bilingual boy, Diego, had horrible speech problems. He missed whole syllables. When he tried to speak, he was very difficult to understand. Thus, it was difficult for Diego to communicate. Karen was worried about him, because the speech therapist had not yet taken him for therapy, and she knew how frustrated and unhappy a child could become in such a situation.

Yet Diego had an abiding happiness and smile that would light up the world.

When Diego came to school in the morning and Karen was on duty outside between 8:15 a.m. and 8:30 a.m., most of the angels would greet Karen with a hug and a "hello." Diego would stand near Karen, waiting for her to notice him. When she did, she would make a fuss over Diego.

"Good morning, Diego. I'm so happy you're here. Give me a big hug!" Then a smile would light up Diego's face, and he would hug Karen and run off to play.

At recess Diego would do the same. He would stand off to the side till Karen saw him, and Karen would smile and say, "Diego, give me a hug." A luminous smile would light up Diego's face as he hugged Karen. Then he ran off to play.

At the end of the class day, Karen determined the order of dismissal. First were always those who had earned awards that day and their tutors. After that Karen varied the pattern. It might be those wearing the color red or those wearing the color black, or those with blue eyes or those with brown eyes, etc.

On this day, Karen said, "If you have shoes that tie with laces, you can walk outside and get your backpack."

Diego, wearing shoes that tied, walked up to Karen and said, "Ooo, ah, oo, oo, ah,"[19] which Karen took to mean, "I have shoes that tie."

Karen said, "Good, Diego." Flashing a brilliant smile, Diego left the room.

Soon Diego got help from the speech therapist and his speech dramatically improved, but his smile did not need improvement. It was already perfect.

---

[19]   Karen could speak Kindergartenease. I would be with an angel for the first time at a center in the beginning of the year, unaware the angel had speech problems, then lean down to hear the angel's words and not understand a syllable. I'd call Karen over to interpret. She would listen as the angel repeated what he had said, comprehend every word, then accurately report what the angel had been trying to tell me. This invaluable skill inured to the benefit of the angels and pleased them immensely. Karen always fought for prompt speech therapy for her angels.

Waiting For Mom

During his first "toy time" of the new school year, a fifteen minute period which the angels enjoy, just before they prepare to go home, a little boy angel, named Aaron, constructed a magnificent structure out of scores of toy blocks.

Karen had just told the angels the toy time rules: play with anything you desire; take turns; when the small bell rings, immediately pick up the toys you have been playing with and return then to where you initially found them.

Karen rang the small bell to conclude "toy time." Aaron quickly dismantled his structure, scattering blocks far and wide, and casually walked away.

Karen quickly said to him: "Aaron, you have to pick up all of those blocks you just played with and put them away."

Unconcerned, Aaron replied: "My mother will be here in a few minutes and she'll clean it up."

Needless to say, Karen quickly set him straight. It never happened again.

A Room Full Of Candy

Karen made out the Sees Candy Christmas order for her campus and portions of others. On this particular afternoon, the order, valued at over $3,500, had just arrived—12 good-sized brown cardboard boxes were wheeled into her classroom on hand trucks. The room was empty, as the angels had left two hours earlier.

Karen started to open and sort the candy into piles to correspond with specific orders, to be delivered throughout the school, or to be picked up by representatives from other campuses, etc. Boxes of candy were piled throughout the room.

Karen ordered as presents, a box of candy for each person on the staff, such as the speech therapist, the principal, the secretaries, the ladies who work in the lunchroom, etc.

Karen delivered a box to the speech teacher.

Three former students stopped by Karen's classroom to say hello.

They then stopped by the speech teacher's office.

Seeing just one box of candy, one of the students said, "You just have one box? You should go in and see Mrs. Brown. She has a whole room full!"

The Stranger

Today a student teacher from sixth grade came down to Karen's room. His name was Mr. Pennington. He came to observe.

When he arrived, Karen was in the middle of a lesson at the blue center. She elected to continue with her lesson and did not interrupt to introduce him. So, Mr. Pennington went to the red center and sat down amid three girl angels who were coloring and pasting.

Mr. Pennington asked one of the little girls, "What is your name?" She would not talk to him. He continued to try to engage the little girl in conversation. She would not say a word to him. She ignored him and completed her work.

Karen rang the bell to conclude the first session of centers so the angels could go to their next center assignments. Mr. Pennington stayed at the red center. The little girl who had rebuffed Mr. Pennington arrived at Karen's center. Karen commenced her lesson with the angels.

After a moment, the little girl angel turned to Karen and said, "Do you see that man over there?"

"Yes," answered Karen.

"He asked me my name, but I wouldn't tell him."

"Oh, you didn't?" asked Karen.

"No. You know, he's a stranger," she said.

"That Thing You Do"

It was 2:30 p.m., the end of the campus school day and the older kids were exiting their classrooms. One of Karen's former students, a boy angel, now a second grader, popped his head into Karen's room, caught her eye and asked: "Are you still doing your thing in here?"

Karen replied, smiling, "Yes, it's called teaching."

"Don't Forget The Liquor"

Early in the school day the angels noticed a parent deliver to Karen a jar of red vine licorice for a surprise snack.

Karen told the angels she would disperse the licorice at snack time.

An hour and a half later, as snack time approached, a little boy angel admonished Karen, "Don't forget the liquor!"

Forgetfulness

Karen noticed she forgot to do something.

As she did so, she said to a boy angel, "Sometimes I forget things."

Concurring, the boy angel replied, "I forget things, too, Mrs. Brown."

Bolero

In December, after recess, I was sitting at the red center alone with a lovely, blonde, girl angel who was completing a coloring task she had not finished earlier during regular center time.

The task was to fill in with color the outline of Santa Claus, which was drawn in blue pencil on white paper.

I watched my blonde charge start coloring. She was using a red crayon. She quickly became engrossed in her work. She never looked up.

After an interval, I thought I heard faint humming. I could not make out a melody.

As she grew closer to completing the coloring, she colored faster and faster, and the humming grew correspondingly louder and louder, until, leaning closer to her, I could finally discern a melody.

It was *"Jingle Bells!"*

Finally, in a coordinated crescendo of coloring and humming, she completed the last few bold strokes with her red crayon, just in time to match the last few notes of *"Jingle Bells."*

"Well done," I told her.

Never looking up, she pushed back her little chair, rose from the table, took her completed work, walked across the room, and placed it into her cubby.

An Autograph

In mid-October, football season, little Damien came into class proudly wearing a San Francisco 49ers sweatshirt.

Seeing this, Karen said to him, "Go 49ers!"

To which little Damien replied, "I play for the 49ers."

Karen said, "Well then, I'll have to get your autograph."

Damien asked, "What's an autograph?"

"That's when you sign your name," Karen replied.

"I don't sign my name that well yet, Mrs. Brown," said Damien, as a matter of fact.

A Thank You

In mid-May one year, the new librarian stopped Karen to speak to her.

She said, "I want to thank you for being so kind to me, so willing to help me in my first year here. I am so grateful."[20]

Karen said, "Thank you," and gave her a hug.

---

[20] Karen was especially kind to new colleagues and staff. Whether it was a new janitor or a new credentialed teacher, Karen, as the self-appointed "Sunshine Person" for 35 years, made extra efforts to make new people feel welcome.

"Did You See Sponge Bob?"

For those readers now far removed from the world of small children and their current cartoon favorites, the immensely popular persona, Sponge Bob Square Pants, is a bright yellow square sponge that lives in the ocean where most of his adventures occur.

During the ten-day spring break in 2010, Karen and I planned to vacation on the island of Hawaii.

Before leaving, Karen told the angels that she and Mr. Brown were going to go to the island of Hawaii in the Hawaiian Islands during spring break. She showed the angels on a world map the mid-ocean location of the big island of Hawaii amid the other Hawaiian Islands.

Easter break ended and school resumed on Monday. On that day Karen told the angels that she had gone to Hawaii and had been able to swim with dolphins. Karen then showed the angels a color photo of her with a dolphin taken at the Hilton Hotel Dolphin Pool.

An angel, Marcos, raised his hand.

"Yes, Marcos?" said Karen.

"Did you see Sponge Bob?" asked Marcos.

"No," Karen answered.

"You know, he lives in Hawaii," said Marcos.

Where Abraham Lincoln Died

In the week of, and before, Abraham Lincoln's birthday, Karen gave the angels a brief synopsis of the life and importance of Abraham Lincoln, to help explain why he is so revered in American life, and forever remembered by the glorious Lincoln Memorial and the national day of celebration to honor his birth.

She told them about his childhood in a log cabin; his love of learning, reading by the poor light of a candle; his prowess as a rail splitter; his exceptional ability as a lawyer; how he became president; how his leadership won the Civil War; how he freed the slaves; his indelible speeches at Gettysburg and at the second inaugural; and how he was killed just after the war ended, shot by John Wilkes Booth at Ford's Theater in Washington, DC.

Immediately after Karen finished, an inattentive angel asked, "Is he still alive?"

Another angel spontaneously responded, "He died at the movies."

"Mrs. Brown Has Vaginitis"

In late May of her next-to-last year of teaching, Karen got a bad cold. She began to lose her voice. As was her habit, she continued to teach. Finally she had to whisper to the angels, "I have laryngitis. I have lost my voice. I will have to whisper."

Karen commenced to use hand signals and occasionally whisper. Irene Gonzalez helped in the morning, as did Karen's aide, who was present from 9:00 a.m. to 10:00 a.m.

On the afternoon of the following day, after the angels had left, the parent of a little girl in the adjoining class, Room 4, appeared in Karen's room to relate the following:

"Mrs. Brown, I just had to tell you this story. We were sitting down at dinner last night. Just as my husband had lifted a fork full of food towards his mouth, our daughter volunteered, 'Mrs. Brown has vaginitis!'"

"My husband's fork stopped in midair. My husband and I exchanged a glance of shocked disbelief."

"So I asked our daughter, 'What do you mean, honey?'"

"She said, 'It's when you can't talk.'"

Karen immediately related this lovely story to other teachers. So for some days to come, whenever Karen passed another teacher on campus, she heard the question, "So, Karen, how's that vaginitis?"

Shopping At Longs

As Karen walked down an aisle at the nearby Longs Drugstore, she heard a woman exclaim, "Oh, Mrs. Woodward! I'd recognize you anywhere. You haven't changed a bit in 29 years. You taught both of my children."

Karen, who had taught under the married name of Woodward until 1994, talked about the former angels, whose names she had remembered.

After a while, Karen and the mother exchanged an affectionate hug and Karen resumed her shopping.

"Remember Me?"

On a May afternoon, long after the angels had left for the day, Karen was working in her classroom when a teenage visitor stopped by.

"Do you remember me? I'm, and I was your projectile vomiter."

Karen thought for a moment. "Yes, I do remember you,. How are you?"

"Well, I am a senior at Arroyo Grande High School, about to graduate."

"That's wonderful," said Karen.

"Do you still have Mr. P. Mooney? I sure liked him."

"Yes," answered Karen, pointing to the two matched cases containing the Peabody Language Development materials that contained Mr. P. Mooney.

After exchanging further pleasantries, they exchanged an affectionate hug, and Karen and her former angel parted.

When Karen came home and told me the story that night, I asked her to explain.

She told me that the poor boy was so upset and distressed that each day, for the first five days of kindergarten, he projectile vomited. On Friday after school, Karen had arranged to meet with the boy and his parents. She explained what had been happening and her empathy for the boy's distress, but stated that something had to change. She could not bear to see the boy continue to suffer, and sadly it also disrupted the class.

Whereupon the father turned to the little boy, pointed his finger at him, and sternly said, "You will not vomit again. It will stop. Do you understand?"

The little boy, wide eyed, nodded his assent.

The little boy never vomited again.

He went on to a successful year in kindergarten, particularly when Mr. P. Mooney appeared.

A Time-Out For Mr. Brown

On the angels' playground, after Carl Daughters died, the school built as a small memorial, a green metal bench, with empty spaces carved out of the back of the bench that spelled the words: "MR DAUGHTERS."

The bench had become, *inter alia*, the spot to temporarily place the various angels who needed to be put into a "time out" for various infractions of the playground rules.

I rarely sat down during the angels' recess periods on the playground, usually passing time pushing the angels on the swings, tying shoes, helping with zippers on jackets, pulling the angels in the wagon, sweeping sand off of the sidewalk, or otherwise watching over the angels.

On this particular day I was tired and sat down for a moment on the then empty DAUGHTERS bench.

Immediately the remarkable angel, Rowland, ran up to the DAUGHTERS bench, sat down next to me, and with his usual breathless exuberance, asked in a loud voice, "Mr. Brown, are you in time out?"

Hearing Rowland's question, but before I could answer, another angel, Xavier, ran up, asking, "Are you in time out?"

Too slow formulating my answer, Rowland asked, "What did you do?"

"Well, actually, I just sat down because I was a little tired," I told both angels.

They both squinted skeptically at me.

A few minutes later, Karen shook her sleigh bells, signaling an end to recess.

I walked over to help the angels form their two lines before entering the classroom. As Rowland got into line, he asked in a loud voice, "Mrs. Brown, did you give Mr. Brown a time out?"

Karen gave me a quizzical glance. I explained what had transpired.

"No, Rowland, I did not give Mr. Brown a time out. He was just resting."

This seemed to satisfy Rowland and Xavier.

Virgins And Vegetables

Karen had commenced teaching the angels about the food groups. She had just discussed the meat food group before the angels went out onto the playground.

On the playground a girl angel approached Karen and asked, "Mrs. Brown, what kind of meat do you like?"

Karen answered, "Well, I don't eat meat. I'm a vegetarian. I only eat vegetables."

The little angel accepted this explanation and skipped off to resume play.

About five minutes later, as Karen walked around the playground near the swings, she overheard her former interlocutor telling another girl angel, "Mrs. Brown is a virgin. She only eats vegetables."

"Mrs. Brown's Boyfriend"

I had visited Karen's class in the morning.

After the angels had gone home for the day, Karen attended a math committee meeting on campus.

One of the angel's mothers attended, who reported to Karen that her child had come home and reported: "Mrs. Brown's boyfriend came to class today."

"Mom Went Wacko."

A little girl angel was coloring at the red center. Karen was walking near her table, when the little girl looked up at Karen, about to speak.

Karen leaned close to hear.

In a matter-of-fact voice, the angel reported, "Mom went wacko last night and tried to kill my grandmother."

Karen hugged the little angel, who then resumed coloring.

Karen waited until recess and referred the matter to Child Welfare Services (by this time, Child Protective Services had changed its name to Child Welfare Services).

A "Fake Believe Owl"

Karen had used the phrase "make believe" to describe to the angels an imaginary item, in this case an owl, whereupon an angel promptly inquired about the "fake believe owl!"

Two Owls And The "P" Sound

Late in the afternoon, the family of a former angel stopped by the classroom with news and a gift for Karen.

The mother of the former angel hugged Karen, told her she loved her, thanked Karen again for teaching her child, and sadly reported that her own mother was dying and that before her death, she wanted Karen to have the gift that the mother was carrying.

The mother then gave the gift to Karen: two ceramic owls.

Karen was deeply moved by the gift.

The two women shared some tender memories of the dying grandmother, who had been deeply involved in her grandson's life while in Karen's classroom. Eventually Karen and the mother hugged again and parted.

Shortly thereafter, the speech therapist came into Karen's classroom with a happy report.

The sweet Down syndrome girl, who was being partially mainstreamed into Karen's classroom, had mastered the sound of the letter "P."

Both women were brought to tears over the little angel's accomplishment.

"Just Like My Mom?"

Karen fielded this question from an angel early in a new school year.

Looking up at Karen with wide inquiring eyes, Cedrick asked: "You're just like my mom, right, only you're at school?."

"I'm your teacher, but I will love you and take care of you when you are here, just like your mother would do," said Karen, smiling down at his innocent face.

Comforted, Cedrick returned to his coloring task.

"Pockets"

Fatima was small for her age, the smallest girl in the class. Also the youngest, Fatima barely came up past my knees. She rarely spoke, and when she did so, it was merely a whisper.

As the angels left through the north door to rush onto the playground for recess, I began to try to talk to her, as Fatima was always slow to get out the door, left in the wake of the bigger, more energetic angels.

I said to her, "Fatima, how are you today?"

I leaned down to try to hear her answer. She reached into her front pockets and turned them inside out, and looking up softly said, "Pockets."

"Yes, I have pockets, too," I said.

I began to count our respective pockets.

"You have two pockets: "one, two," I said, pointing first to her right front pocket and second to her left front pocket.

"Let's see how many pockets I have," I said. Fatima's eyes followed as I counted:

"One," I said, pointing to my right front pocket.

199

"Two," this time pointing to my left front pocket.

"Three," turning so Fatima could see, pointing to my left rear pocket.

"Four," turning so Fatima could see, pointing to my right rear pocket.

"Five," pointing to the breast pocket on the left front of my long-sleeve white shirt.

Satisfied with the exchange, Fatima ran off to play.

Throughout the fall, Fatima and I shared scores of exchanges of "pockets." I would see her in the cafeteria, in the classroom, leaving for recess, during toy time, at centers, walking to the library, walking to the computer lab, on the bus during a field trip—and she would point to her pockets . . . and I would point to mine . . . and we would both say or mouth the word, "pockets."

As the year developed, Fatima began to thrive as she mastered her letters, sounds, shapes, and colors. We eventually came to enjoy brief conversations, but it all started with the simple sharing of "pockets."

Postcards From Hawaii

Karen has been traveling to Maui annually since approximately 1973, and she acquired a timeshare there in 1978, giving her two weeks every July.

Every trip she made to Maui, she took the addresses of her most recent class and mailed to each angel a handwritten, personal greeting on a postcard.

In 2008, on an afternoon, a former angel, now an adult and a parent herself, stopped by to see Karen. They exchanged excited greetings and hugs.

The now adult angel said, "You know, Mrs. Brown, I still have that postcard you sent to me from Hawaii when I was in your kindergarten."

Zen Boy

Alex smiled nearly constantly. It was a dazzling smile. Beneath his bowl cut, jet-black hair with bangs, his pure white teeth, set off by his olive complexion, he illuminated Room 1. He was the happiest child.

Alex had won the parent lottery. He came from a loving family.

Nothing fazed Alex. He carried himself with an overriding calmness, no matter what the situation. He seemed serene.

Alert to the smallest of things, Alex was easily distracted by such things as: a paper dropped onto the floor, a passing classmate, a remark from another table.

When Alex was directed to go to a center, or to get his backpack, or to assume his role as line leader, or to fulfill his role as morning weather person, he often seemed not to hear, so intent was he upon some other distraction. Multiple cues were often needed to get his attention. When that happened, he smiled his brilliant smile and got on task.

Walking alongside Alex, near the middle of the hot lunch line, en route to the cafeteria, late one morning, I observed a monarch butterfly carve a jagged path as it passed from right to left above Alex. Alex stopped dead in his tracks. He watched the butterfly, until it passed out of sight around a corner of the nearby principal's office, oblivious to the 30-foot gap that had opened in the lunch line.

Reluctantly, I interrupted his reverie, and tapping him on his right shoulder, I said: "Alex, get going, catch up." Smiling his dazzling smile, he hurried to close the gap.

An ancient question then occurred to me: Was Alex a butterfly dreaming he was a boy, or a boy dreaming he was a butterfly?[21]

I had the utter pleasure of observing this lovely situation more than once, as about a mile away, in a grove of 100-foot tall eucalyptus trees, thousands of monarch butterflies pause twice each year during their multi-thousand mile, migratory trek to and from their winter home in a remote valley in Mexico.

I miss Alex's dazzling smile and his gentle ways.

---

[21] In the 3rd century BC, the Chinese philosopher Chuang Tzu wrote: "Once Chuang Chou dreamt he was a butterfly, a butterfly fluttering around, happy with himself and doing as he pleased. He didn't know he was Chuang Chou. Suddenly he woke up and there he was, solid and unmistakable Chuang Chou. But he didn't know if he was Chuang Chou who had dreamt he was a butterfly, or a butterfly dreaming he was Chuang Chou. Between Chuang Chou and a butterfly there must be *some* distinction. This is called the Transformation of Things." *Chuang Tzu, Basic Writings,* translated by Burton Watson p. 45, Columbia University Press (1964).

"Help Yourself"

In Karen's first week at Grover City Elementary, a little blond girl, whom I'll call Amy, not her real name, was consistently picked up at the end of class by a waif like blond girl Karen assumed to be the teenage babysitter.

Early the next week, a scruffy looking man, who identified himself as Amy's father, picked her up from school. Later that week, it became apparent to Karen that Amy had some behavior problems, so she wanted to speak to the mother, who was presumably raising Amy.

So on Friday of the second week, Karen spoke to the teenager, who again came to pick up the little girl: "Could you please ask the mother to contact me, as I need to talk with her about Amy?"

Surprised, the waif stepped back saying: "I'm her mother!"

"Oh," said Karen. "You're so young, I thought . . ."

Cutting her off, the young mother asserted, indignantly, "Well, I'm 19!"

Soon thereafter Karen and the mother had a talk and developed a rapport. Karen then began incidental checking for any further background information that might help her understand the child and her circumstances. She heard rumors that the father was more than likely involved in the sale of illegal drugs.

At the first Parent Teacher Conference, Karen and the mother were alone in Room 1. After a lengthy conference about Amy, the mother began to ask Karen questions about class size. When Karen said she had 38 students, the mother wondered how Karen could possibly handle the stress. The mother said her three children (aged 5,3 and 1) drove her to distraction.

Karen replied that she had to be very organized and did have help from her team teacher, but agreed that it was very stressful.

The mother then opened her large black purse, showing the contents to Karen, saying, in a kind voice: "This could relieve some stress. Help yourself."

Karen observed what she assumed were a number of marijuana cigarettes (Karen has never smoked marijuana) and various small, clear plastic bottles, with white screw caps, each containing different colored pills.

"Thank you," said Karen, "but I'll just try to get along."

"Mr. Alien"

A volunteer named Mr. Allen came to help in the classroom to teach music.

He was introduced to the angels as "Mr. Allen."

A short time later, little Kaitlin asked Karen, "Where's Mr. Alien?"

Go Big Red

Karen told the angels she was going to go to Nebraska to visit some of Mr. Brown's relatives.

To which an angel inquired, "What's a Nebraska?"

Testing

Although Karen's foundational language system, the Hawaii English Project, is so specific she knows from day to day the status of each angel, in February of each year Karen is required to formally test each angel to assess academic progress.

Since the opening day of school, the angels are made to notice and to state the specific day of the week. Early on, they also learn the days from the *Days of the Week* song.

Karen sat down beside her test subject, a little angel who had been in class continuously since day one.

She said to the angel, "Say the days of the week."

The angel innocently replied, "The days of the week."

As Karen told this story to me, my immediate reaction was to recall that scene in the classic Mel Brooks movie, *Blazing Saddles*, where the evil state attorney general, Hedley Lamarr, played deliciously by Harvey Korman, stands in a dark, three-piece suit atop a high desert rock, before a band of the meanest thugs he could find, all mounted on horses. He intends to deputize them before they are sent to destroy the town of Rock Ridge to drive out the townspeople so that the railroad can route itself through Rock Ridge. The following dialogue occurs:

Hedley Lamarr: "Raise your right hand and repeat after me." (A number of left hands are raised.)

Hedley Lamarr: "I."

The thugs, in unison, all say, "I."

Hedley Lamarr: "Your name."

The thugs, in unison, all say, "Your name," and Hedley Lamarr rolls his eyes to the heavens.

Our story has a better ending. When I questioned Karen about the actual results of the testing after that initial, literal exchange, she said that the boy angel knew all of his shapes, colors, letters, both large and small, and the sounds the letters made. He did wonderfully.

Karen concluded there must have been something odd about the manner in which she posed her initial question that caused such a literal answer.

Evan And Van Leave School

Karen's last class was blessed with two twin boys, Evan and Van.

They were uncommonly kind, gentle souls.

On the playground, more than once, I had seen Evan and Van give the ball they had been playing with to another boy for a turn. They were unusually unselfish for so young an age. They were honest, loving and completely without guile.

Late in the year, Evan and Van had to leave Grover Beach. They were moving to the Pacific Northwest, where their father had taken a new job. On their final day, the angels stood at their places on the carpet and Evan and Van walked down each line, giving hugs to everybody.

I was sad to see them go.

The Politician

While enjoying a mid-summer meal at a local restaurant, Karen was approached by an attractive, outgoing, petite, blonde waitress to communicate her excitement that her daughter, Sky, was enrolled in Karen's next kindergarten class. In August, when Sky arrived at school, she was the image of her mother—beautiful, blonde and effervescent.

Starting the first full week of class and continuing for the entire school year, each angel got one turn per week to bring an object to class for sharing. Karen, sitting in her chair in front of the angels, who were arrayed in four rows on the rug, called forth a sharing angel who arrived and stood next to Karen, holding a brown paper bag containing the item to be shared.

The angel was to give three clues, request up to three guesses, and after the item was identified, solicit three comments.

Most angels were initially quite shy, often trying to hide behind Karen. Some angels initially would not bring an item for sharing in order to avoid the public speaking aspect of it. The angels tended to look down into their brown paper bags and mumble their clues. Karen usually had to repeat the clues so they could be heard and repeatedly prompt the angels to call on three guessing angels and, after the item had been identified, on three commenting angels.

Not so with Sky.

She walked confidently to the front of the class. In a loud voice, she gave her three clues, saying, "It is shaped like a rectangle. My sister is on it. I am on it."

Sky called on a classmate. "Is it a lunch pail?"

"No," said Sky.

Sky called upon another classmate. "Is it a book?"

"No," said Sky.

She called on another classmate for the final guess. "Is it a picture?"

"Yes," said Sky as she removed from the bag the framed photo of Sky and her sister in a happy pose. Then Sky proudly displayed it for all the angels in the class.

Sky easily fielded three comments, which were the usual. "I like it. It's cool. Where did you get it?"

After class, Karen spoke to Sky's mother to tell her how remarkably poised and confident Sky had been during sharing time.

Her mother said, "You know what? She's going to be a politician. I just know it."

"So Gwad To See You"

Christopher was truly an angel. An extremely sweet, kind and loving boy, he brought light to the darkness that often surrounded him.

Christopher exhibited the problems of a child who had been exposed *in utero* to drugs: poor self-control, hyperactivity, difficulty staying on task, and speech problems. His mother lived in Arizona. His father was also absent.

His maternal grandmother was raising Christopher, until she died in a car wreck. An aunt intervened to care for Christopher until his mother, still occupied with her own recovery, returned from Arizona, moved into her mother's home, and commenced to care for him.

One day when Christopher returned to kindergarten after an absence, he greeted Karen, saying, "I'm so gwad to see you."

Karen gave him a hug. "Christopher, I'm so glad to see you, too."

Karen provided such a safe, structured, positive, loving environment that Christopher soon thrived and successfully graduated to first grade.

Twin Day

One day each month is devoted to a special activity. Sometimes the day is denominated "crazy hat day". Sometimes it is "pajama day". This day was "twin day". The idea was to get together with another classmate and dress as identically as possible.

Karen and Carl Daughters always joined in this spirited activity and conspired to dress alike. This day they both wore black jeans, black tennis shoes and identical, dark blue, Grover Beach Gopher sweatshirts. Karen wore a white baseball hat, her blonde ponytail sticking out through the back of the hat. Carl wore a white baseball cap over a faux blond wig. Carl had two pair of sunglasses with the lenses punched out. He wore one and gave Karen the other.

Thus attired, they entered the classroom. Carl initially pretended to be Karen. Karen initially pretended to be Carl. The angels loved it.

Then Karen and Carl commenced the regular classroom day.

A little girl angel then noticed something. "No. No. You're not exactly alike, because you have earrings and Mr. Daughters does not."

"You're right. That's true. He is not wearing earrings, so we're not exactly alike," said Karen, complimenting the angel.

Another boy angel said, "Look, your ring is different than his ring."

"Yes, that's right," confirmed Karen.

Then another observant boy turned to Karen and said, "And you have breasts and he doesn't."

A Suspicious Man

Walt Wald, an excellent teacher who loved kids, taught fifth grade. A lifelong surfer, Walt still had a lot of the little boy in him. He dressed too casually, often wearing jeans and a T-shirt to school. His hair, seldom cut, grew full and frizzy, making him resemble Bozo the Clown.

Early one morning, before school had started, while dressed in jeans and T-shirt, sunglasses and a baseball cap that did little to contain his frizzy hair, Walt stood on the south playground field, chatting with some of his students.

A police car drove by, glanced at Walt, and called the school office to report a suspicious man on the south playground. The principal, secretary, and custodian immediately ran towards the playing field to search for the suspicious man.

The police officer had already exited his vehicle, and when the principal and his posse reached Walt, he was engaging the officer in conversation. Seeing the obvious, the principal vouched for Walt. All was well.

Then Walt had to enter his classroom and explain to his students why the police had questioned him.

To Snow Or Not To Snow

In January each year, Karen rented a truckload of "snow" (several tons of crushed ice) from a local ice company so the angels could frolic in "snow," usually for the first time in their young lives.

During the week scheduled for the snow, Karen primed the angels with anticipation, which included requesting that each angel bring, if possible, a dollar from home to help pay the ice company for the snow; a warm coat; boots and gloves.

On Thursday, the day before the snow was to arrive, Karen reminded the angels about the snow event planned for Friday, choosing as her opening words, on a typically cloudless, bright sunny day, "We are going to have snow tomorrow."

To which a boy angel volunteered, "You know, the weatherman always lies!"

A concerned girl angel immediately added, "I don't want to waste my dollar!"

"Taking Home The Snow"

Every January, Karen made arrangements with a local ice company to deliver and dump onto the grassy area of the kindergarten playground, a truckload of crushed ice, so that the angels could have a "snow day".

The angels greatly anticipated this event. They planned in advance to wear a warm coat, boots, and to bring gloves.

The kindergarten angels got to play on the snow all morning. After they left school, the older kids played in the remaining snow.

On this day, after Karen's angels had their fill of the snow and were preparing to go home, a little girl angel returned to Room 1, wearing her backpack, and went to her cubby to get her take-home materials.

It was then that Karen noticed two wet spots that corresponded with the placement of the little girl's front pockets. So, Karen asked the little angel why her pants were wet.

"Mrs. Brown, I'm taking home the snow."

The Weatherman

Every January Karen arranged for a truckload of crushed ice to be delivered to the kindergarten playground, which sat just a mile from the surf line of the Pacific Ocean, so the angels could experience the artificial California equivalent of snow.

Most of the angels had never seen real snow, or been able to wallow in the snow, or to make a snowball, or a snowman. The January "snow" delivery let them do all the above with glee.

On Monday Karen announced that it was "going to snow" on Friday and told the angels they would need gloves or mittens, warm coats, hats, and boots, if possible.

Karen further said she had talked to the weatherman and he had assured her that they would have snow on Friday.

On Friday about 10:00 a.m., as the angels watched from inside the classroom, a dump truck loaded with "snow" backed onto the kindergarten playground.

One of the angels then asked Karen: "Is that the weatherman driving the truck?"

Show And Tooth

On a fall afternoon after the angels had gone, a former student, now a first grader, stepped into Karen's classroom.

Walking up to Karen, the angel opened his mouth and wiggling his tongue over a lower front tooth, proudly exclaimed: "Look, I've got a loose tooth!"

Snake Sharing

A little boy angel walked to the front of class and stood next to Karen for his turn at show and tell, carrying a white shoebox with holes poked into the closed lid.

He placed the box on Karen's lap and gave three clues:

"It starts with the letter 's.' It's alive. I found it in my yard," he said.

Karen's heart began to race.

The first guess scored. "Is it a snake?"

"Yes," said the boy.

Karen now knew she was in trouble.

Keeping the box on her lap and the lid between her and the contents, Karen lifted the lid. A mad garter snake rose up, hissing right at Karen. Petrified, Karen smashed the lid back down. She commenced to shudder amid muffled sounds of hissing.

Holding the box with an iron grip, Karen quickly rose from her chair, walked across the rug to the cubbies and placed the angry snake above the cubbies, out of reach, saying, "We'll leave this up here until Mr. Daughters comes back."

Carl had been out of the room during the commotion. When Carl returned, Karen told him about the hissing snake and how afraid she had been. "Oh Karen, you're making a mountain out of a molehill," he teased. So Karen told Carl to go see for himself.

Carl casually walked over to the shoebox and lifted the lid. The snake shot up to its full height and hissed in Carl's face. Carl slapped the lid down. The entire transaction took about two seconds.

He returned to Karen. "I see what you mean," he said.

Show And Tell Cocaine

The sweetest little girl angel, whom I'll call Christy (not her real name), came forward at her sharing time and stood next to Karen, holding in front of her a closed brown paper sack. She gave these clues: "It's made of glass. It starts with the letter 'b'."

"Is it a bear?" an angel guessed.

"No," said Christy.

"Is it a baby?" another guessed.

"No," answered Christy.

"Is it a book?" a third angel guessed.

"No," said Christy.

"That's three guesses, Christy. Since no one guessed correctly, show the class what you brought to share," said Karen.

Christy pulled from her sack a clear glass vial, about three inches tall, sloped at the shoulders, containing a half inch of white powder settled at the bottom, secured with a cork stopper. Christy next removed from the paper sack a small silver spoon. Christy showed these objects to the class without comment.

Karen, in her innocence, had no idea it was cocaine.

Christy then solicited three comments, the most important one of which was: "Where did you get it?" an angel asked.

"From a coffee table at home," Christy replied.

Christy's sharing then concluded, and she put the sack containing the cocaine and spoon into her cubby. Carl Daughters quietly pulled Karen aside a few minutes later to tell her that the bottle likely contained cocaine and the spoon was a needed implement as part of the process by which addicts measure and/or cook the cocaine.

Carl then removed the sack from Christy's cubby, telling her it was needed in the office for safekeeping. A CPS report was made.

Later, a CPS worker reported to Karen that the parents claimed they had "no idea" where the stuff had come from. Christy was not removed from the home.

Sharing Tooth Stories

A boy angel came forward during his sharing time.

His sharing was, "I lost a tooth," pulling down the front of his lower lip to show his fellow angels the missing space.

As this display was occurring, another boy angel volunteered, "My dad lost all his teeth in a bar fight."

As usual, the angels absorbed this remark without judgment or comment.

"Old Mcdonald's"

A boy angel, whom I'll call Jeff (not his real name), came forward to the front of the room, holding his paper sack for his turn at sharing. He stood next to Karen and gave these clues: "It starts with the letter 'd.' It's black. It comes from a DreamWorks movie."

The first guess: "Is it a dog?"

"No," answered Jeff.

The second guess: "Is it a deer?"

"No," said Jeff.

The third guess: "Is it a dinosaur?"

"Yes," said Jeff as he removed it and displayed it to the class, a movie tie-in toy from a Happy Meal at McDonald's.

It was time for three comments.

The first angel's comment, "That's really cool."

Second angel's comment, "Where did you get it?"

"Old McDonald's," said Jeff.

Second angel, with a follow-up question, "The place that has the fries?"

"Yes, and burgers, too," answered Jeff.

Sharing A Roach Clip

It was sharing day for little Ben (not his real name). He came forward and stood next to Karen holding his brown paper bag.

Without looking into his bag, he gave two clues: "It's metal. It's small." (No third clue) The angel's three guesses were ineffectual, so Ben removed the item from the bag.

Karen had no idea what it was, but Mr. Daughters practically ran from the back of the room to take possession of the item, thanking Ben for his sharing.

"Where did you get this, Ben?" Carl asked.

"From the kitchen table," he replied.

Later Carl told Karen it was a roach clip, used to smoke marijuana.

Another report was made to CPS.

Show And Tell Too Much

It was time for Mary (not her real name) to share.

She walked to the front of the room and stood on Karen's right. Karen was seated in her chair, facing the angels, sitting in rows before her.

Mary pulled apart the edges of her paper bag, looked inside and gave three clues: "It starts with 'K'. It has my name on it. You can put your keys on it."

It was time for her classmates to guess.

"Is it a keychain?" an angel guessed.

"Yes," said Mary.

The angels then got to make three comments.

"Where did you get it?" an angel asked.

"My dad brought it back from Arizona," Mary answered.

A month earlier, while picking up Mary from school, her father had told Karen that his company, which installs solar systems, was sending him to New York and then to Arizona for temporary work.

So Karen, intending to show the angels that Mary's father worked and sometimes worked out of town said: "Mary's father has an important job. He installs solar collectors so that people can have heat and light."

Mary then volunteered: "He doesn't do that anymore. The cops took his truck away. He was drunk and driving."

As usual, the angels accepted this revelation without comment or judgment.

The Blitzkrieg [22]

Karen has long had a love affair with Dachshunds.

A shorthaired, red female Dachshund, eight weeks old, arrived when Karen (nee Blackburn) was about nine years old and living in San Bernardino. The dog was a purebred. Her mother had been named Blanche. Her father had been named Dinkie. Thus, her registered name was Blackburn's Binkie.

For a Dachshund, Binkie was sweet and gentle. Binkie bonded with Karen. They were inseparable. Sadly, when she was only one year old, Binkie contracted distemper from a neighbor dog and died. Karen was distraught.

Seeing Karen's sadness, in less than two weeks her brother, Gary, purchased another shorthaired, red female Dachshund puppy, also about eight weeks old, which Karen quickly named Binkie.

The second Binkie was also sweet and mellow. Karen bonded with Binkie. By then Karen lived in Huntington

---

[22] The term Blitzkrieg—German for "lightening war"—was coined by journalists after the invasion of Poland by Germany in September, 1939, to describe the German's quick victory due to the simultaneous use of combined arms, consisting of dive bombers, tanks, mechanized artillery, and infantry, with concentrated, overwhelming force and rapid speed. I called this story the Blitzkrieg solely because of the aspects of surprise and speed, not to promote any war-like references.

Beach. Karen and Binkie went everywhere together. Binkie loved tug-o-war and chasing tennis balls. Binkie frequently walked with Karen to nearby Bolsa Chica Beach, just a half mile across a tomato field behind Karen's back door.

After Karen turned 16, she drove her 1956 Chevy and Binkie rode in her lap. When Karen went away to college to Cal Poly in San Luis Obispo, Binkie would climb into her suitcase, hoping to go with her. Both Karen and Binkie cried real tears each time they parted, but the reunions were joyous.

In 1971, when Karen married, Binkie went with her. Binkie and Karen were together 17 years. Eventually, Binkie had to be put down after her kidneys failed. Karen grieved for Binkie.

A month later, Karen was fixing dinner at her home in Arroyo Grande, listening to the radio. An announcement said that two Dachshunds, a male and a female, located at the local pound in San Luis Obispo, were to be put down within 24 hours, if not adopted. Without checking with her husband, Karen rushed to the phone, called the radio station and said she would take the female. The person at the other end said they would alert the pound of Karen's intentions.

Karen got into her car and rushed to the pound, which was just past the California Men's Colony off of Highway 1, a few miles west of San Luis Obispo.

Karen rushed in the door and said to the man behind the counter, "I've come to get the female Dachshund that was mentioned on the radio."

The counter person asked Karen, "Do you want to go back and see her first?"

Karen said, "No, just bring her out," as Karen intended to keep the dog, sight unseen.

The man behind the counter left and soon reappeared walking a black Dachshund on a leash into the room.

Karen exclaimed, "Oh, she's black," having always had red Dachshunds.

Since Karen is like a kindergartner and does not notice the color of a person's skin, it was only then that Karen noticed that the man who had been helping her was a black man!

The black man's expression darkened, "Oh, so you don't want her now?" he asked.

"Oh, no, of course I want her. I only noticed she was black, because all of my other Dachshunds were red. I am so sorry to have said that. Please forgive me," gushed an embarrassed, red-faced Karen.

All was well, and Karen filled out the paperwork for her dog. It was then that the man told Karen that her new Dachshund had been the pet of an elderly man who had died alone. The Dachshund had stayed with her deceased master for three days until the authorities found the man with the Dachshund sitting on his chest.

When Karen put her new Dachshund into her car, the frightened dog jumped between the front and back seat, wailing. Soon Karen started the car and talked the dog into her lap, petting her and saying soothing things to her. As she drove the 20 miles back to Arroyo Grande, Karen decided to call her new dog Miranda.

Karen and Miranda slept together that night and for months thereafter. Karen and Miranda bonded. But for about a year, whenever the front doorbell rang, Karen thought that Miranda seemed to be looking for her former master. Once when Karen had a portly houseguest with a big stomach, Miranda wanted to sleep on his stomach. Karen surmised that Miranda's former master must have been portly.

Miranda turned out to be Karen's sweetest dog. She wanted to cuddle all the time. She was friendly to all comers and never barked excessively. Miranda always cooperated with whatever Karen wanted to do. Karen came to believe that Miranda knew that she had been rescued and was grateful.

About six months after we were married, I had to take Miranda to the vet to be put down. Miranda's kidneys had failed. Karen and Miranda had then been together for 14 years. Karen wept as she said good-bye to Miranda. My own tears fell on Miranda as I cradled her in my lap as I drove her to the vet.

Karen was very sad after Miranda was gone. Within a week, Karen started looking for a new Dachshund. We found one in Santa Maria and brought her home, another red female. Karen named her Miss Money Penny[23]. Karen took three days off school (unheard of for Karen) and spent every minute with Penny. Penny, who was tiny, slept on Karen's neck, so Penny could feel a heartbeat. Thereafter, Penny and Karen were bonded for life.

Penny turned out to be a classic Dachshund. Feisty, barking at everything, always charging at other dogs, wanting to pick a fight, barking at kids on bicycles, barking at anyone on a motorcycle, impossible to train. Karen spent $300 on a trainer. As a result, Penny would sort of heel if you jerked up on her leash hard enough. She would not sit. She would only squat. She refused to go all the way down to the pavement, apparently as a matter of principle.

She had us both trained to do anything she wanted. Last year we had the stairs to the second story tiled, and Penny had no traction on the stairs. So, Penny had us carrying her to and from the second floor at her whim.

---

[23] Penny suffered a rapid decline and died in my arms in January of 2011.

So it came as a fitting surprise early one spring afternoon after the angels had gone, when a fellow teacher walked into Karen's classroom to ask a question. In so doing, she left the front (south) door open.

In ran a young red male Dachshund. He dashed around the corner of the credenza, turned right, ran onto the rug, circled the rug, ran into the angels' bathrooms and back, ran into the rear storage area, ran back out onto the carpet, rounded the toys and turned left towards Karen, who was now standing behind the yellow center next to her computer chair. Karen called out, "Hello, little boy," and reached down towards the red raider.

Hearing Karen's voice, the Dachshund ran to Karen, wagging furiously, and stopped to allow Karen to pet him, then rolled onto his back so Karen could pet his stomach.

Then quick as a flash, he jumped up and raced out of the classroom.

Dogs are not allowed on campus. In Karen's 37 years no dog had ever gotten into her classroom.

I like to think the dog's visit was a salute to Karen, a victory lap, done on behalf of all the Dachshunds Karen had loved and cared for over the years.

How fitting.

On Patrol

Wienerdude daily takes Jesse for a mid-day walk, counterclockwise, on the sidewalk around the eight-block circumference of Grover Beach Elementary.

Chocolate brown, sleek and shorthaired, Wienerdude is handsome: a seven-year-old boy Dachshund in the prime of his life. Jesse, his alleged master, is a senior citizen in his twilight years.

Wienerdude disdains a leash. He walks point, way out ahead of Jesse. Every so often, Weinerdude looks back and waits for Jesse to close the gap that has opened between them. Weinerdude then resumes patrol.

Wienerdude is serious. He ignores distractions, especially children. When Wienerdude and Jesse reach the eastern edge of the kindergarten playground on the Longbranch Street side, walking tangent to the chain-link playground fence, a knot of angels forms at the fence. The angels then inscribe an L shaped arc as they follow Wienerdude along the 150' Longbranch Street fence line to the corner, Wienerdude turns south along the 100 foot 10th Street side of the kindergarten playground, until the playground fence cuts away from 10th Street at the parking lot exit. All the while, the angels are calling out to Wienerdude try to get his attention.

Wienerdude ignores the angels. He sniffs the sidewalk.
He sniffs the rectangular patch of earth between the sidewalk
and the curb. He sometimes looks across the street, away
from the playground. He never looks at the angels, not even
in their general direction.

If Wienerdude encounters anyone approaching on
the sidewalk he ignores them. It is not possible to pet
Wienerdude. He is on patrol. He is working.

When Wienerdude reaches the school parking lot, if it is a
warm day, he will sometimes pause under the shade cast by
the front fenders of the cars parked nearest to the sidewalk.

The only time Karen had a chance to meet Wienerdude
occurred on a sunny weekend morning when she and
I were visiting her classroom, about two months before
Karen retired. They met on the sidewalk at the base of the
parking lot. Wienerdude looked up and stopped. Karen
started talking to him and bent down to pet him. Wienerdude
collapsed into wagging wiggles of happiness as Karen
fawned over him.

After that happy interval, Wienerdude resumed patrol,
walking ahead of Jesse.

A Loving Family

Ally, a girl angel in Karen's class, came from a most loving family.

On Ally's birthday she wore a birthday crown and stood smiling next to Karen in front of the class while her fellow angels honored her with a loud chorus of *"Happy Birthday."*

When the song ended, Ally announced, "My mom said to me this morning that the day I was born was the happiest day of my mom's life."

While Ally was still in kindergarten, her mother and father rescued by adoption a three-year-old boy who had been in an abusive home.

Not long after that, her mother and father took in a developmentally disabled girl with terrible motor problems. As of this writing, that angel is now in the developmentally disabled class just around the corner from Karen's former kindergarten.

Ally and her brother and sister will have full lives, blessed by their loving family.

Capital Letters

Stephen, a sweet little boy, had ADHD, Attention Deficit Hyperactivity Disorder. Thus, through no fault of his own, he had a hard time concentrating and staying on task.

Karen had been working and working with Stephen to recognize the capital letters.

Stephen got frustrated and said to Karen, "Mrs. Brown, I just can't do this!"

"Oh, I know you can, Stephen. You can do it. I know you can. You just have to practice," said Karen, encouragingly.

Stephen then said, "You know, really, I'm just not that smart."

(He did learn his capital letters and a lot more, and got help with his ADHD.)

"Isn't This Beautiful?"

Andy (not his real name) was an autistic boy placed in Karen's class, because she had a special ability to connect with the disabled.

Due to his disability, Andy had a flat manner, devoid of verbal or facial expression. He came to school daily. He seemed to tolerate the class well. Karen hoped, but could not tell, if Andy had the capacity to enjoy.

Valentine's Day is an important day in kindergarten. It is the first time that the angels get to exchange a valentine with a peer. Karen provided bags that the angels decorated with multiple hearts and hung on the front of their cubbies. Karen then provided the angels with enough valentines to distribute to each classmate. The angels then placed a valentine into each bag.

On Valentine's Day the angels take down their bags from their cubbies, sit down on the rug, open their bags, and see their valentines. Each angel will have at least 20-30 valentines. It is a happy time.

Karen paid special attention to Andy as he opened his valentines. He opened and read each card from his fellow angels. Andy was an exceptionally good reader. He read the valentines over and over.

He finally looked up at Karen and said, smiling, "Isn't this beautiful?"

It was the first smile Karen had ever seen from Andy, and it and he were beautiful.

A Priceless Gift

On Valentine's Day, Karen received a priceless gift.

A little girl angel had gone to the thrift store and bought Karen a gift, a ceramic birdhouse.

As she handed it to Karen, her eyes moistened with tears as she proudly proclaimed, "Mrs. Brown, I bought this with my very own money!"

The birdhouse, marred with many nicks and chips, still displayed a ten-cent price tag.

"Oh, honey, that's the most beautiful gift I have ever seen," Karen gushed, her own eyes tearing.

Karen immediately put it at the front of the room next to her chair as she told the class how beautiful it was, and that she was displaying the beautiful birdhouse for everyone to see.

"Cwap"

A little boy angel, whom I'll call Bobby (not his real name), could not yet produce the "l" sound. Bobby was sitting at the green reading center with Karen and six of his classmates.

"Mrs. Brown, my Uncle Tony can cwap," he volunteered.

Initially unsure of what Bobby was trying to communicate, Karen was nervous about following up with a question, so she elected a neutral response: "I know your Uncle Tony."

"And you know about his TV?" asked Bobby.

"No," Karen replied.

Bobby then slapped his small hands together, creating the sound of a single clap, saying, "He cwaps and the TV comes on, and he cwaps and the TV turns off."

"So Whose Birthday Was It?"

To celebrate the birthday of her longtime teaching aid and dear friend, Irene Gonzales, Karen ordered a sheet cake from Costco that would feed all three kindergartens. I picked it up and brought it to Room 1.

At the appointed time, all 80 kindergartners gathered together in a circle on the playground. Irene Gonzalez went into the middle of the circle and they all sang "*Happy Birthday*" to her. While in the circle, she opened all of her presents, while all the teachers served plates of birthday cake to the assembled angels.

When everyone was finished with his or her cake, and Irene had opened all of her presents, it was time for half of the kindergarteners to go home.

Karen then encountered a little boy named Salvador leaving the playground with his mother. With crumbs from the birthday cake still clinging to the corners of his mouth, he asked, "So whose birthday was it?"

No More School?

In her third year of teaching kindergarten, Karen encountered a little boy whom I'll call Charles (not his real name).

Charles had a hard time learning how to write the letters of the alphabet facing the right direction, and to write his own name. Finally in May, after much individual attention, Karen saw Charles correctly write his own name and all the letters of the alphabet.

Karen immediately praised him: "Charles, I'm so proud of you. You can write your name now!"

"Wow. So I don't have to go to school anymore?" asked Charles.

"Oh, no, honey, you go to this school till sixth grade, then you go to junior high, then you go to high school," Karen replied.

"Gee, my mom said all I have to do is sign my name to get welfare," said Charles.

First Day Excitements

At the end of the first day of kindergarten, Karen recounted for the angels all the fun things they had done that day.

"We made a Gingerbread Man cookie. We chased the Gingerbread Man all over the school. We ate a Gingerbread Man cookie. We ate in the cafeteria. We played on the playground. We played with toys. We sang our '*Good Morning*' song and our '*Good-Bye*' song."

A little boy then volunteered, "And we washed our hands."

A Form Of Peanuts

Little Noah (not his real name), when asked to choose a snack, replied, "penis," pointing to the can of peanuts, his favorite snack food.

Hard Feelings

On the opening day of a new school year, a young mother delivered a beautiful daughter to Karen's class. The little angel had a wonderful first day.

At 12:30 p.m. the mother returned to pick up her daughter. Before she left the classroom with her daughter, the mother pulled Karen aside for a few words.

"I don't ever want you to mention the word 'father' in here," she said.

Aghast, Karen firmly told the mother that she was the teacher; she could never agree to any form of censorship; nor would she agree to the mother's request, as it was utterly unreasonable. She urged the mother to keep such thoughts to herself.

The Kid

A boy angel in Karen's class, whom I'll call Billy (not his real name), had a retarded father whom I'll call Bob (not his real name). Bob could not work, so Billy's mother worked to support the family. Bob stayed home and supposedly took charge of Billy.

Billy was in the afternoon class, which ran from 11:30 a.m. until 2:45 p.m. The afternoon class went to the cafeteria at noon where Billy, like most others in class, qualified for a free lunch. Bob initially accompanied Billy to and into the cafeteria, but after he was observed eating from Billy's tray, Bob was promptly and permanently ejected from the cafeteria.

Bob complied and thereafter waited for Billy outside the cafeteria. Then he would accompany Billy to the kindergarten playground where the angels enjoyed 15 minutes of playtime before re-entering the classroom. Bob happily played with the kids, swinging, using the slide, the seesaw, sometimes kicking the soccer ball.

When Karen stepped onto the playground and jangled her sleigh bells, the angels knew to pick up their toys and quickly form a double line, line leaders in front, before being directed to enter the classroom. Bob would wave at Billy as he entered the classroom. Bob then headed home.

For the last 15 minutes of the school day, from 2:30 p.m. to 2:45 p.m., the angels gleefully enjoyed "toy time" in the classroom. The angels had a thousand nearby items to choose from: scores of puzzles and board games, boxes of blocks, boxes of Legos and Lincoln Logs, scores of toy cars, scores of toy trucks (fire, semi-trailer, dump, oil tankers and pickups;) ten toy earth-moving equipment tractors, scores of airplanes, a dozen Barbie and other dolls in the dollhouse, two giant pirate ships and boxes of pirate gear, toy parking garages, houses, and barns, 200 bookshelf books and a play kitchen with 250 pieces of toy dishes, food and flatware and furniture, a baby cradle filled with stuffed animals, and eight computers assembled and programmed with games by Mr. Daughters.

To pick up Billy, Bob would always arrive early for "toy time." Bob joined in with the angels. He happily played on the computers, played with the puzzles, and sometimes played with the big trucks, taking turns with the angels.

After 15 minutes, Karen would ring a shrill silver bell she kept on her desk, which signaled the angels to quickly clean up. Bob did not like to stop, as he was having too much fun; nor did he like to clean up after himself. Karen let it pass once, but no more. So, she admonished Bob. "Bob, when that bell rings, EVERYBODY cleans up, even you." Thereafter, Bob complied.

Billy, like too many of Karen's angels, exhibited the effects of attention deficit. He could not attend to a task. Too often Billy was in the wrong place at the right time or the right place at the wrong time, yet he was so sweet, gentle, and kind that all were drawn to him.

One day, remarkably, Billy was the first to clean up after "toy time" and return to sit quietly on the rug. Karen immediately praised Billy and rewarded his behavior by directing him to go and select a prize from the "prize box."

"Billy, come and get a prize from the prize box," Karen said to Billy.

Of course, Bob had been present. He rushed over, beat Billy to the prize box, and began rifling through the box. The "prize box," a clear plastic container, about two feet wide, three feet long, and six inches deep, contained hundreds of new trinkets, like new pencils, stickers, erasers, and small toys.

After a few minutes, Billy held in his hand the prize he wanted, a brand-new pencil painted in iridescent colors. Bob had already made another selection, a Disney toy from McDonald's. "Hey, Billy, get this," he urged.

"No, Dad. I want this," Billy replied.

Seeing this, Karen quickly endorsed Billy's choice.

A few minutes later, just as the kids were about to leave the classroom, Bob cornered Karen and asked, "If I bring a dollar, can I have that prize out of the prize box tomorrow?"

In January, Karen arranged her annual snow day where a ton of ice from a local ice company is deposited from a dump truck onto the kindergarten playground, forming a mound of "snow." On this day, Bob appeared and quickly became "king of the hill," too vigorously repelling the assaults of kindergarteners to dislodge him. Several teachers asked him to get off, but he ignored them, so Mr. Daughters quickly intervened and removed Bob from the playground.

By the time June arrived, Karen had little patience left for Bob despite her compassion for his obvious childlike condition.

Karen did an Hawaiian unit in May that ran into June. The angels learned about everything Hawaiian, even some Hawaiian language. Karen also taught the angels how to sing and dance the Hukilau. For the finale of the Hawaiian unit, the angels performed the Hukilau for their parents in full costume, previously made in class, then enjoyed a luau party in the classroom.

After days of practicing the Hula in the classroom, Karen and all 80 kindergarteners went to the cafeteria for a final rehearsal the day before the performance. Karen stood in front of the angels, all in their stocking feet, going through the music and motions of the Hukilau.

Karen soon noticed that some of the angels were snickering. Karen NEVER got this reaction from her angels, so she turned around just in time to see Bob conclude a mimicking Hula movement. Treating him like the child he was, Karen barked, "Bob, you are going to have to leave if you don't behave yourself!"

Bob responded with a childish attempt at an alibi: "I wasn't doing anything. It wasn't me. I didn't do anything." But he immediately stopped. The rehearsal and the resulting program were a great success.

Billy, of average intelligence, managed to master the basics and graduate to first grade, but Karen had a hard time selecting the right placement for Billy. There were at that time four 1st grade classrooms.

Two were bilingual. Billy would not thrive in a bilingual classroom, because it would be too hard for him to wait while the Spanish speakers received their instructions, before he got his. Men taught the two remaining 1st grade classes.

One man was in his 60's and could not deal with a hyperactive child. The other man had such a laissez-faire attitude that his classroom had virtually no rules. The class was chaotic, but it was the only place Billy could go. Sadly, because Billy and all the angels thrived in Karen's well controlled yet positive, loving classroom.

The following September, after the second day in the chaotic 1ˢᵗ grade classroom, Billy stopped by Karen's room.

"Mrs. Brown, do you think you could come to 1ˢᵗ grade to help me?" he plaintively asked.

Karen hugged Billy, then said, "Oh, Billy, I am so sorry. I can't come and help you, honey. I have all these new kindergarteners that need my help now. I'm not going to be able to be with you like last year."

"Oh . . . okay," said Billy, resigned.

He turned and walked away.

Kindergarten Candy

In 1921, Mary and Charles, See commenced See's Candies in Los Angeles, California. Their delicious chocolate confections quickly became famous in California, and so popular throughout the country that in 1972 Warren Buffett added the company to his Berkshire Hathaway empire. An emblem of the company is a black-and-white cameo of a grandmotherly Mary See.

About 1977, Karen's second year of teaching, See's Candies sent a flyer to Grover City Elementary, offering a discount to teachers for the placement of an order exceeding $500. Karen saw a flyer. As the "Sunshine Person" on campus, Karen asked around and immediately solicited from the other teachers an order of over $500.

Over the next three decades, Karen was the See's Candy contact. As Grover Beach teachers transferred to other schools, they would collect on-campus candy orders and place an order from the new school through Karen. Word spread. Teachers representing other nearby campuses called Karen to place orders for their respective schools. Karen's total See's order usually exceeded $3,000. Karen did all the work on her own time and at her own expense. Karen never removed a dollar from the monies she collected. No profit was ever made by Karen, only by See's.

The boxes would arrive at kindergarten in the afternoon after all the angels had gone. Karen would sort the orders by destination. The off-campus orders would be picked up immediately that day or by the end of the following day. Karen immediately distributed the Grover Beach orders.

In late November a sixth-grade student, a sweet girl, had asked Karen's permission to come to her classroom after 2:30 p.m. to assist, but essentially to be with Karen. Karen had cleared it with the girl's parents. The girl was present in early December when she observed a delivery man wheeling a hand truck, delivering boxes into Karen's classroom. It took three trips to deliver about a dozen boxes.

Karen did not allow the angels to ever have candy in the classroom, on their person, or in their backpacks, with the exception of the occasional jellybean she awarded for excellent work or behavior. Karen is unique in that she refused to allow her students to select chocolate milk in the cafeteria, and demanded that her angels select a piece of fruit from the buffet at every lunch.

As Karen opened the large boxes, the young girl could see that they contained many smaller, rectangular boxes wrapped in identical red Christmas paper. Karen began sorting the boxes according to destinations: Fairgrove Elementary (formerly North Oceano), the District Office, and Harlow Elementary. The rest went to Grover Beach.

The young girl asked Karen, "What's in the boxes?" Without looking up, Karen said, "See's Candies."

Shocked that this was for Karen's students, the little girl, frowning, admonished Karen, "You know, Mrs. Brown, when I was in kindergarten, we weren't allowed to have candy!"

Mr. Brown Plays The Guitar

At the time mentioned, Karen had team taught kindergarten with Carl Daughters for 17 years. Carl frequently led the angels in song as he played his guitar. Karen and Carl got on so well that the angels had a factual basis to support their constant belief that Karen and Carl were married.

In January, a new girl from Michigan arrived and greeted Karen and Carl in kindergarten. During her first day, Carl, strumming his guitar, led the angels in song. Apparently when the new girl returned home that day, she told her mother all about her new kindergarten, about how much she liked Mrs. Brown and her husband, who played the guitar.

When class ended the next day, the new girl's mother arrived to take her daughter home.

The mother asked Karen, "Oh, did your husband, Mr. Brown, come in and play the guitar?"

"No, I don't believe he plays a musical instrument," Karen literally answered.

"Well, my daughter told me that he had been in to play the guitar," she replied.

Then it dawned on Karen that the mother was talking about Mr. Daughters. Karen then explained that Mr. Daughters was her teaching partner of many years, and it was he who played the guitar.

Cold Hands

Karen has endured cold extremities all her life, probably related to untreated thyroid issues. Her hands are always cold to the touch.

Frequently, Karen has wrapped her frigid fingers around an angel's penciled hand, helping to form correct letters.

This day Karen was holding a little boy angel's hand, helping him to write a small sentence. The boy asked, "Mrs. Brown, how come your hands are always so cold?"

Karen said, "Well, I just have bad circulation."

"I will blow on them if you want me to," he offered.

"The Piano"

One of Karen's boy angels, turning six years old, hosted a big birthday party. The week of the birthday, he delivered invitations to all members of the class for the party to be held that Saturday.

On the following Monday, the boy told Karen he had a "piano" at the party.

Karen remarked, "Oh, my goodness. Did you all stand around and sing? What did you do with the piano?"

"No. We hit it with a stick," he explained.

"You hit the piano with a stick?" asked Karen?

"Yes, and you hit it real hard and some candy falls out."

Then it dawned on Karen. He meant a piñata, not a piano.

"The 'G' Word"

This day a new student, a little girl whom I'll call Mary (not her real name), arrived in class, having previously attended a private religious school.

Early in the day, Mary took her place at a table with four other angels engaged in a task of coloring. Shortly thereafter, Mary raised her hand.

Karen recognized her, "Yes, Mary?"

"Mrs. Brown, that boy right there (pointing at the offender) said the 'g' word."

Karen's mind quickly raced through her limited vocabulary of off-color words, then had to ask, "Well, honey, I don't know what that word is."

"You know . . . he said, 'God,'" Mary explained.

Karen's investigation quickly discovered that the offending boy, a meticulous lad, had invoked God immediately upon discovering he had colored the wrong spot on his paper.

Karen then said to Mary, "Well, honey, if that bothers you, all you have to do is say to him, 'Please don't say that,' and he won't say it again."[24]

---

[24] That solution was true to Karen's constant attempts to empower the angels to be assertive in their personal relationships. From the beginning and throughout the school year, Karen told the angels to first address a classmate directly, telling him/her to stop doing behavior that offends. Karen even gave the angels a script. She told them to say, "Please stop. I do not like that." Then if the offensive behavior did not stop, to immediately tell Karen and she would quickly intervene.

"The 'C' Word"

Karen was on playground duty one morning, before the start of class, when a girl angel rushed up to her and said breathlessly, "Mrs. Brown, that boy over there said the 'c' word!"

Karen, in her innocence, did not possess a large prurient vocabulary, so it took less than a second for her mind to race through any obscene words she knew that started with the letter "c."

So she questioned the angel further. "He said what word?"

The angel repeated, "He said the 'c' word."

"Well, honey, I don't know what the 'c' word is," admitted Karen.

Irritated, the little girl said, "You know . . . shit!"

"One Nation Under Dog"

During the daily Pledge of Allegiance, Karen tried to stand in a different spot each day.

One time in April, Karen stood next to Jane (not her real name) who was the largest girl in the class, over four feet tall and weighing over 100 pounds.

By this time in April, the angels had recited the Pledge of Allegiance over 150 times.

When the angels reached the phrase, "One nation under God," Karen heard Jane say, "One nation under dog."

A Pledge Of Allegiance

The angels first encountered the Pledge of Allegiance in kindergarten. It took them some time to learn the ritual and the words.

Starting on the first day of school, Karen directed the angels in their first Pledge of Allegiance.

Karen selected a flag person for the week. She asked the child to come forward to the front of the rug, and to face the class. She told the flag person to say to the class, "Please stand."

The angels, arrayed on the rug in four parallel rows, all stood.

With all the angels standing, Karen then told everyone to turn towards the small flag, displayed eight feet high on the wall just above and to the right of the angels.

Generally in unison, the angels executed a quarter turn to the right and looked up at the flag. (Karen and the flag person turned 90 degrees to the left.)

Karen then placed her right hand over her heart and told the angels, "Now place your hand over your heart." Each angel seemed to place a hand, often a left hand, in the general vicinity of the upper torso.

Karen had the flag person say, "Ready . . . begin."

Karen then led the "Pledge of Allegiance."

As she did so, she observed the angels. It was then that she noticed a boy in the back row facing the flag, proudly reciting the Pledge, with his right hand clasped firmly to his crotch.

A "Grief Case"

During toy time, Christopher was playing in the playhouse where items of clothing were available with which to play.

Christopher emerged from the playhouse with what appeared to be a purse on his arm, and proceeded to walk across the classroom.

Karen said to Christopher, "Oh, my goodness! You have a briefcase. Are you going off to work?"

"Yes," he answered, and took a few steps further.

Another angel, Blake, walked up to Christopher and said, "Christopher, you can't carry a purse!"

To which Christopher replied, "That's not a purse. That's my grief case!"

The Jellybean Caper

Starting early in the school year, the Parent/Teacher Association determined to use box tops as a yearlong fundraiser. Apparently box tops, returned in bulk, could generate cash.

When Karen announced the box top program, she offered to give out one jellybean per box top. This proved to be successful.

Some angels never brought in a box top. On several occasions, Karen noticed an angel with five box tops sharing them with four of his classmates so that five angels could each get a jellybean. The commercially produced box tops were uniform: postage stamp in size and red in color.

One little girl angel never brought a box top, but she had the best small motor skills in the class. Whenever she had a coloring project, her finished product was so beautiful it looked as if had been produced by a professional.

One morning this talented little angel handed Karen a "box top" that she had created from scratch, simply from observing the other box tops as they had been submitted. It was an accurate and lovely forgery.

Karen accepted it with a wink and handed the smiling angel a red jellybean.

A Best Friend

One morning Karen asked the angels: "If you could pick anyone to be your best friend, who would it be?"

A little boy angel responded, "Mrs. Brown. She could be my teacher for about 100 years and be my best friend."

"Don't Leave Me Alone"

An officer from the Grover Beach Police Department annually visited the classroom to speak to the kindergarteners about safety issues.

The officer, in full uniform, would talk to the angels about the dangers of talking to strangers and how to run from one if threatened; how to dial 9-1-1 in the event of an emergency, such as a fire in the house; how to stop, drop, and roll in the event they were ever on fire; to never touch a gun, and to report the presence of one immediately to an adult; how to repeatedly look both ways when crossing a street, and the location of marked crosswalks for that purpose; to be careful about approaching dogs they encountered outside of their own homes; and to report to a teacher immediately if they were being bullied, etc.

The police officer would then respond to questions, most of which had to do with the gear he was wearing, especially his badge and gun.

The presentations normally lasted 15 minutes to correspond with the attention span of a kindergartner.

This day a new officer, a female, was replacing the male officer who had been doing the presentations for the previous years. The lady officer was in full uniform, including a loaded side arm, mace, baton, handcuffs, and extra clips of ammunition.

When she entered the classroom, she quickly went to Karen, pulled her aside, and in a panicked voice, whispered: "Don't leave me alone with them!"

An Autistic Boy Speaks

Allen (not his real name) was an autistic boy who had a flat affect. He never emoted or seemed excited about anything. He avoided physical contact with others. He never engaged anyone in conversation.

One morning he earned an award, because he had identified all 225 flip cards in a Reading Word Comprehension (RWC) section of the Hawaii English Project.

At the end of the day, Karen led the entire class in applause for each angel who individually came forward to receive their awards from Karen.

When Allen's name was called, he smiled broadly, bounded forward, exclaiming, "I did it! I did it!" and as Karen, who was sitting in her chair, handed him his award, he hugged her and kissed her on the cheek.

In all of Karen's years in the classroom, that was the only time an angel ever kissed her upon the receipt of an award.

A Sad Report

At the reading center during a brief lull, a little girl angel whom I'll call Rose (not her real name), sitting right next to Karen, volunteered: "My mom doesn't live with us anymore."

This sad report was presented as a matter of fact. If other angels overheard it, they absorbed it without reaction or comment.

Over the years the angels had made many such poignant reports to Karen.

Later on the playground, Karen hugged Rose and told her everything would be all right.

A Pee Story

The angels had the luxury of their own bathrooms in the back of Karen's large kindergarten classroom. The little toilet seats were only ten inches off the ground.

Tommy (not his real name), the front of his pant legs obviously wet, came up to Karen to complain: "Stephen (not his real name) peed on me."

"Where were you?" asked Karen.

"In the bathroom," replied Tommy.

"Were the two of you in the bathroom?" Karen asked suspiciously. (One of the bathroom rules was only one at a time.)

"I went in to see if someone was in there," explained Tommy.

Karen then marched Tommy into the bathroom and found Stephen, whose pants were dry.

Karen asked Stephen, "Were both of you in here at the same time?"

"Yes. It was a mistake," answered Stephen.

Karen further questioned Stephen, "Did Tommy get wet while you were in here?"

Stephen said, "Yes. It was a mistake. I was going potty and Tommy came in to talk to me, and I turned to talk to him and he got wet."

"A Real Pain In The Ass"

Robert (not his real name), like too many of Karen's angels, had been exposed *in utero* to drugs and had all the symptoms of ADD. It was not his fault that he could not concentrate, even for short periods of time, and thus could not finish a normal kindergarten task without repeated redirection.

At the end of 15 minutes at a center, Robert left the center and showed Karen his work. It was not done. So Karen took Robert back to the center, handed him a box of crayons, and pointed out the specific sections of the single assignment page he needed to complete.

As she finished, Karen was surprised to hear Robert say, not in a mean way, but more out of exasperation: "You know, Mrs. Brown, you're a real pain in the ass."

Robert went directly to time out, eventually finished coloring the page, and a note went home to his caregivers about Robert's unfortunate use of language, which never happened again.

The Date

A sweet boy angel, Kevin, surprised Karen one April morning.

"Mrs. Brown, could you go to see a movie with me?" he asked. He then named the specific movie he wanted to see, and said it would be shown on April 28th.

This was a first for Karen, but she said: "Well, if it's ok with your mother, then yes."

Later Karen spoke with Kevin's mother, who confirmed that Kevin had discussed the idea of asking Karen to go to a movie with him, and she had agreed that it was okay if that was okay with Mrs. Brown. Karen then told Kevin's mother that she would go to a movie with Kevin.

On April 27th Kevin again spoke to Karen in the classroom. He said: "Mrs. Brown, the movie isn't till May 5th. Can you be flexible?"

Charmed, Karen said: "Sure, May 5th will be fine?"

On My 5th I accompanied Karen to the Arroyo Grande multiplex theatre for the matinee. There she met Kevin and his mother, who purchased three tickets. I followed the party just inside the theatre door to take a picture of Karen and her date.

I decided to squat to get a better camera angle and as I did so, Kevin also squatted. Then Karen got down on one knee and I took their picture, which, sadly, I have lost. But the sweet memory remains.

"Big Daddy School"

At Karen's green reading center, she listened as five angels discussed how much they liked school. Karen then told the angels that she still went to school to take classes on Saturdays, and at night to learn to be a better teacher.

A little boy angel then volunteered, "My dad still goes to school, too. He goes to big daddy school."

"Does he go to Cal Poly or Cuesta College?" asked Karen innocently.

"No. He stole a car and they sent him to big daddy school," he said.

As usual, the angels absorbed this revelation without reaction or comment.

Abalone

The school librarian, Piper Adelman, sees the angels once per week when they visit the library. Piper's gentle, soft-voiced manner, her effective use of inflection, expression and timing, mark her as a master storyteller. The angels are enthralled when, to conclude every library visit, she reads or tells them a story.

On this day, Piper had a large abalone shell, the interior so highly polished it gleamed like a jewel.

Piper told the angels about all things abalone—how they live in the sea, many just off our nearby coast; how they are a source of food for others; how in the nearby dunes "middens" were discovered, representing thousands of abalone shells discarded in a great pile, hundreds of feet tall, by the local Indian tribes hundreds, even thousands, of years ago; and how abalone are now scarce and protected, and only harvested by special permit, and only if they are large enough. The angels were then allowed to see the gleaming shell.

After the story ended, the angels rose from the carpet and formed two lines at the library door. Karen then did what she always does.

"All right, class, let's all say, 'Thank you, Mrs. Adelman.'"

An angelic chorus then followed Karen in saying, "Thank you, Mrs. Adelman."

"Now let's blow her a kiss," said Karen.

The angels mimicked Karen as she touched her right hand to her lips, flung her arm outward to full length, like tossing a Frisbee, and exclaimed, "Waagh!"

The angels turned right out of the elevated modular classroom and down the ramp. While walking down the ramp, a boy angel next to Karen said to her, "You know, Mrs. Brown, a bologna lives in the shell and you can reach in and get the bologna and make a bologna sandwich."

Librarian Piper Adelman and the abalone shell

"Do You Sleep With Mr. Daughters?"

For Back to School Night, Karen prepared with each angel a multi-paged packet entitled "All About Me," stating each angel's name, school, number of family members, favorite colors, and toys. One page contained a small space for the angels to draw a small picture of their bedroom and the bed they slept in.

As he started drawing a picture of his own bed, a boy angel asked Karen, "Mrs. Brown, do you have your own bed, or do you sleep with Mr. Daughters?"

"The Other Mrs. Brown"

I had been going to Karen's kindergarten daily for months. I had usually arrived at 9:00 a.m. and had stayed until after 11:00 a.m.

During that time, I had helped at a center, usually the red center, from 9:00 a.m. to 9:30 a.m.

From 9:30 a.m. to 9:45 a.m., as I had watched Karen read the angels a story, I had tied various angels' shoes. (At any one time, about 25% of the shoes in the class were untied.) I had then assisted with snacks. I had squirted a bit of hand sanitizer onto the outstretched palms of the angels, and then had helped pass out snacks. (I often passed out too large a helping of a particular snack, underestimating the size of the angel's hands or the length of time they needed to eat the snack, and Karen often had to correct me.) Then I had gone to the drinking fountain at the sink and had helped the angels select a manageable water flow from the plastic fountain attachment, and offered a paper towel. The girls took the paper towels. The boys preferred their sleeves.

From 9:45 a.m. to 10:00 a.m., the angels spilled out onto the playground. On the playground I had pushed the angels at the swings, had tied more shoelaces, had pulled angels in the wagon, had played catch with a ball, and had generally observed. Sometimes I had to put an angel into a time out.

From 10:00 a.m. to 10:50 a.m., tutoring occurred. I had tutored selected angels on shapes, on colors, on small letters, on capital letters, and on same/different identification, with a goal of finishing a task and getting the angel a much sought after award. A few times Karen let me read to the angels. I had always chosen *The Cat In The Hat*, for its lovely rhythm and rhyme.[25]

At 10:50 a.m. the angels lined up for lunch. Hot lunch angels in one line, cold lunch angels in the other. I had deposited another round of hand sanitizer onto the palms of the angels, and then had helped monitor the angels on their trip to the cafeteria.

In the cafeteria I had helped the hot lunch kids load their plates, get their napkins, spoons, and straws, and get seated at the table. I had helped the cold lunch kids; had opened their drink cartons, delivered needed napkins, or peeled hard-boiled eggs, etc. I had then returned with Karen to her classroom where she would eat her lunch.

The angels were eventually taken from the cafeteria by one of the Spanish-speaking ladies, who walked the angels back to their playground and watched over them while they played until 11:30 a.m., when Karen would ring her sleigh bells and the angels would re-enter the classroom for the final part of their school day.

---

[25] I always intended to expose the angels to Kipling. I thought they would have loved the musical rhythms and rhymes of *Rikki-Tikki-Tavi;* but sadly, I never got around to it.

After about four weeks of doing the above, I got a very bad cold and had to stay away from the classroom for ten days. When I first returned, I made a brief visit to the playground after the kids had returned from lunch, and I left just before Karen rang the sleigh bells at 11:30 a.m.

After Karen rang the sleigh bells and a line formed, one of the angels in line said to Karen, "The other Mrs. Brown was here. Did you see him?"

"Hot Lunch?"

When Karen walked the angels over to the cafeteria for lunch, she would lead two lines. The shorter line was for the cold lunch angels. They brought their own lunches with them in paper bags or lunch boxes. The hot lunch angels formed the much longer second line.

The cold lunch angels entered the cafeteria first, turned immediately left, and took their seats at the long first table.

Karen stayed long enough to see that the angels successfully got through the hot lunch line, making sure they got white milk (never chocolate), a fruit, a vegetable, requested condiments, and a spoon/straw/napkin pack, wrapped in cellophane.

Karen then joined the angels at their long lunch table. She helped with spills, dropped food, and special requests, like a need for ketchup, or ranch dressing, or another napkin packet, or help opening a juice packet, or a milk carton, or a fruit package from home. (Karen always urged the angels try to be assertive: to open their own milk cartons and other containers, to help them develop self-confidence and small motor skills).

Karen and I would then walk back to Room 1, where Karen would eat her own lunch during what remained of her paltry 15-20 minute lunch break. I would then go off campus to get some food and return for the remainder of the school day.

Early in the year, I had gotten to know a little boy angel, whom I'll call Bobby, not his real name. Bobby was seldom picked up on time at the end of the day. Since his caregiver was chronically late, I got to spend a lot of time talking with Bobby. After waiting 15 minutes in the classroom, I would then walk Bobby to the office, where I would leave him. The office staff would then telephone his caregiver. Bobby was open, verbal and enthusiastic. He had a buzz cut and I always patted him on the head when I left him.

One day I accompanied Bobby and the other cold lunch kids into the cafeteria and helped them get seated. I was standing behind Bobby as he opened his peanut butter and grape jelly sandwich. Bobby then looked up at me. He seemed concerned. He asked: "Mr. Brown, you getting hot lunch today?"

"Sure," I said.

An Angel's Mite[26]

At the end of a school year a boy angel named Anthony from one of the poorest families came into class with his mother.

The mother told Karen, "He made a gift especially for you to thank you for all you have done for him during the school year. He wants you to have it."

The little boy, eyes expectantly wide, held up and handed to Karen a small white box the size of a deck of cards. It was a used Sucrets throat lozenge box.

Karen opened the box. Inside, wrapped in toilet paper, she found a plastic token from the local Chuck E. Cheese, a chain of pizza places in California that offer arcade games. With the token, Karen could go to Chuck E. Cheese and play a game.

---

[26] The Widow's Two Mites

Now Jesus sat opposite the treasury and saw how the people put money into the treasury. And many who were rich put in much. Then one poor widow came and threw in two mites, which make a quadrans. So He called His disciples to Himself and said to them, "Assuredly I say to you, that this poor widow has put in more than all those who have given to the treasury; for they all put in out of their abundance, but she out of her poverty put all that she had, her whole livelihood." ((*The Bible*: Mark 12: 41-44; (King James)).

Smiling and trying not to cry, Karen hugged the token to her chest and exclaimed, "Oh, Anthony, that is the most wonderful gift I have ever received!" Karen meant every word.

She hugged Anthony, who beamed with happiness.

The Death Of Mr. Daughters

The phone rang.

It was just after sunset on a Monday evening in November of 2004, the end of a three-day Veteran's Day weekend. I was sitting on the black leather living room sofa, looking to my right out through a wall of windows as the setting sun turned the underside of a slab of gray stratus clouds lingering above the dunes, bright orange.

"Hello," I answered.

It was a friend of Carl's, a fellow pilot, whom Karen and I had recently met at lunch with Carl and Sue.

"Carl and Sue are way overdue. They should have landed at the Santa Maria airport hours ago. They are coming back after visiting relatives in Arizona."

I thanked him for his call. He said he would keep us informed. He had already alerted the FAA.

I trudged upstairs to deliver the ominous news to Karen. We talked for about a quarter hour. Then I returned downstairs. The stratus clouds were now a deep purple, as the evening had "spread out against the sky, like a patient etherized upon a table;"[27]

The following morning, I had just situated both my clients in the gallery of Department 4 of the Superior Court in San Luis Obispo, anticipating their separate hearings, when my cell phone vibrated. I quickly left the courtroom and entered the hallway to take the call.

"Hello?"

It was Karen, sobbing: "Carl . . . is . . . dead . . . please come."

I quickly arranged for a colleague to make appearances for me to continue my hearings to a future date, hurriedly explained the emergency to my clients, and raced to the Palm Street parking garage to get my car. I was in Room 1 in 25 minutes.

Through tears, Karen explained that she had earlier been called to the office to take a call. It was from Carl's daughter, Anna, who lived nearby in a Grover Beach mobile home park. Anna broke the news that a search and rescue crew had reached the crash site in the Sierra Nevada Mountains. Both Carl and Sue were dead.

---

[27]   T.S. Eliot, *The Waste Land And Other Writings*, *The Love Song of J. Alfred Prufrock*, p. 3, Modern Library Edition (2002)

There followed a blur of activity, culminating days later with a public memorial service for Carl at the new Clark Center for the Performing Arts in Arroyo Grande. The Clark Center, aptly named after local benefactors, Clifford and Mary Lee: Clark, occupies the northwest corner of the Arroyo Grande High School campus, tangent to Farrell Road on the north, Valley Road on the west, the vast Arroyo Grande High School parking lot on the east, and modular classrooms to the south. The interior amphitheater seats 750. It was standing room only when I ascended the steps to the stage to speak on Karen's behalf, as she sat sobbing in an aisle seat three rows from the stage.

"I am the real Mr. Brown. (Small nervous laughter) The little ones always thought Carl and Karen were husband and wife. Whenever Carl first introduced his wife, Sue, to the class, most of the little ones looked askance at her. The same reaction greeted me whenever Karen first introduced me to her class."

"Last August, Carl and Karen commenced their 25th continuous year together, team teaching kindergarten in Room 1 at Grover Beach Elementary. They truly lived those years among the angels, the little Kindergartners placed in their loving care."

"My first glimpse of the beautiful world Carl and Karen inhabited occurred in January of 1995, just a few months after Karen and I had married, when I made my first visit to Room 1. I had come directly from court, unannounced, so I was dressed in suit and tie. When Karen saw me, the angels were arrayed on the rug at her feet. Carl was in the back of the room, working on computers. Karen immediately must have recognized an opportunity for a guessing game."

"So in that animated way that got and held the angels' attention, Karen exclaimed: 'Oh look . . . we have a visitor . . . who could this be?'"

"A hand was raised. Karen called on a little boy angel: 'Is he a policeman?'"

"'No,'" said Karen.

"Another hand was raised. Karen called on a little girl angel. 'Is he a judge?'"

"'No,'" Karen replied.

"Karen called upon a third angel who had raised his hand. 'Is he your probation officer, Mrs. Brown?'(A gale of laughter swept through the audience). 'No, Mrs. Brown doesn't have a probation officer,' explained Karen."

"Finally, a girl angel frantically raised her hand. Karen called upon her. 'I know! He's Martin Luther King, Jr.!' (Happy laughter from the audience). Karen, Carl and I exchanged quick glances."

"There was one black angel in the class, a boy, whose hand immediately went up. Karen called on him. (Later the adults compared notes. We all thought he would point out the obvious, that I was white and Dr. King was black). The little black angel announced in a loud voice: 'That can't be Martin Luther King, Jr. He's dead!'" (Laughter filled the theatre).

"Karen then introduced me as her 'husband,' the 'daddy in her house'. I was met with quizzical stares as I sat down on top of the low table that I would later learn was the pink center. A few minutes later, when the morning class left for the day, three girl angels veered in my direction, to hug me on their way out of class."

"Carl and Karen lived among the angels. Here are more examples."

"A little girl angel approached Karen on the playground during recess and breathlessly exclaimed: 'Mrs. Brown, _____ used the 'C' word!' Karen quickly reviewed her limited vocabulary of prurient words and came up empty. So she leaned down to the angel and asked: 'Well, honey, exactly what 'C' word do you mean?'

"To which the little angel impatiently replied: 'Well . . . you know . . . shit.'"

(Laughter filled the auditorium).

"Early in the school year, Karen used a hand puppet, Mr. P. Mooney, who had his own happy song, a magic stick, and an apron Karen wore when Mr. P. Mooney appeared on her hand. Karen used Mr. P. Mooney to teach the angels language skills, including how to introduce themselves."

"In that drill Karen would sit on her chair in front of the angels, who looked up at her from their places on the rug. Holding Mr. P. Mooney in her right hand, she would ask Mr. Daughters to come forward and introduce himself to Mr. P. Mooney. Carl would walk up, shake right hands with Mr. P. Mooney, while saying: 'Hello Mr. P. Mooney. My name is Mr. Daughters.'"

"Karen would then direct each angel to walk up to Mr. P. Mooney and shake right hands with him while saying: 'Hello, Mr. P. Mooney. My name is _____.'"

"One time when Karen did this exercise, there were 35 angels in the class. One of them was a sweet little black boy named Donald, whose language was street language, omitting various sentence parts. So Karen had Donald go last. After having the language correctly modeled by the prior 34 angels, Donald briskly walked up to Mr. P. Mooney, gave him a round-house high five and exclaimed: 'Yo . . . P. Mooney . . . I be Donald.'" (More laughter).

"One of the first things the angels do daily is salute the flag. The angel who has been designated the flag person for the week, comes forward to face the class, places his/her hand over his/her heart, and then says, 'Ready'. And as the angels seem to be placing their hands over their hearts, then he or she says, 'Begin' and recites the Pledge of Allegiance.

"In April one year, after the angels had correctly saluted the flag about 100 times, Karen noticed that when the flag person put her hand over her heart to commence the Pledge of Allegiance, everyone in class followed, except a boy in the back row, who was saluting the flag with his right hand cupped firmly over his crotch." (More laughter).

"During the first week of school, Karen read to the angels different versions of *The Gingerbread Man*, wherein the gingerbread man encounters different characters during his successful escape. As Karen reread a version, the gingerbread man was about to meet a cow. To encourage and to test the angels' ability to listen and remember, she said to the angels, who were assembled before her on the carpet: 'Turn to your neighbor and whisper what you think will happen next.'"

"Little Giovanni, who spoke mostly Spanish, was sitting in the front row. He was not whispering to anybody, so Karen leaned down to him and said: 'Whisper something to me.'"

"Little Giovanni whispered: 'I think you're beautiful'" (Laughter and applause).

"Early in September, Karen and Carl helped the angels fill out a single page of personal data, to which the angel's picture would be attached. These biographical sheets would be displayed on the kindergarten walls until Back to School Night. The angels would then find their bio sheets on the walls, and have their parents take them down and take them home."

"One of the questions on the bio sheet was: 'What do you want to become when you grow up?' Most boys answer 'policeman' or 'fireman.'"

"Artie was the smallest boy in the class. When Karen asked Artie what he wanted to do when he grew up, he responded: 'A motorcycle racer, Mrs. Brown, but only after I get training wheels.'" (Laughter).

"Karen and Carl were simpatico. They were in agreement on how to teach, how to structure the classroom, and how to create safe and secure boundaries for the angels in their loving care. They welcomed the hard cases, ones others could not handle. They reached angels others could not reach. The disabled were always mainstreamed into their classroom, because they were so welcomed and the environment was so safe, secure and loving."

"Now to honor Carl's love of flight, the poem *"High Flight,"* by John Gillespie Magee, Jr.[28]

---

[28] Frances Bretano, *The Questing Spirit, Religion In The Literature Of Our Time,* also edited by Halford E. Luccock, *High Flight,* pp. 316-317; Coward-McCann, Inc. (1947).

'Oh! I have slipped the surly bonds of earth,

And danced the skies on laughter-silvered wings;

Sunward I've climbed and joined the tumbling mirth

Of sun-split clouds—and done a hundred things

You have not dreamed of—wheeled and soared and

swung

High in the sunlit silence. Hov'ring there,

I've chased the shouting wind along and flung

My eager craft through footless halls of air . . .

Up, up the long delirious, burning blue

I've topped the wind-swept heights with easy grace,

Where never lark, or even eagle, flew;

And, while with silent, lifting mind I've trod

The high untrespassed sanctity of space,

Put out my hand, and toughed the face of God.'

"And now to borrow from Shakespeare, Horatio's lament upon the death of Hamlet: 'Good night, sweet prince, and flights of angels sing thee to thy rest.'"[29]

Post Script:

Seven years later, as I was writing this chapter, I was telling Karen about John Gillespie Magee, Jr.: how the 18-year-old poet had been accepted at Yale, but because of his English heritage (his mother was British), he left

---

[29] William Shakespeare, *The Globe Illustrated Shakespeare, the Complete Works, Annotated,* Edited by William Stanton, illustrated by Sir John Gilbert; *Hamlet,* Act V, Scene II, p. 1922, Gramercy Books, Random House Value Publishing (1979).

America for Canada and completed pilot training with the Royal Canadian Air Force in 1940; how in June of 1941 he had been posted to England in an RCAF squadron; how in September, he composed *"High Flight"* in his head during a high altitude test flight; and after landing completed the poem that day on the back of an envelope; and how, just three months later, on December 11,1941, he died in a mid-air collision with another British plane on a training mission. He was only 19 years old.

After I had finished, Karen said: "You should have used his poem, *"High Flight"* at Carl's memorial service."

I was stunned. "I recited the entire poem! You didn't hear it?"

"No. I guess I was so sad. I didn't hear a word of it," she replied.

Memorials

Two memorials on campus commemorate Carl.

The bench was the first.

On the eastern edge of the sandy area containing the angels' playground equipment, looking permanently west towards the setting sun, workmen bolted to a cement base a forest-green metal bench, with the name "MR DAUGHTERS" cut out of the back rest.

Days later the entire school assembled on the kindergarten playground to dedicate the bench. Karen was too sad to go outside, but she remembers the assembled singing Carl's favorite song: "The World Is A Rainbow."[30]

The World Is A Rainbow

---

[30] *The World Is A Rainbow*, words and music by Greg Scelsa, *We All Live Together*, volume 2, Youngheart Music Education Service, pp. 16-17 (Copyright 1978).

The World Is A Rainbow, p. 2

At the end of the song, Carl's green memorial bench was unveiled on the edge of the playground, permanently facing the swings, the slides, the ocean and the setting sun.

Carl's Memorial Bench

The Carl Daughters Learning Center came second.

Dedicated in the following year, the Carl Daughters Learning Center (the campus computer lab) occupied modular classroom #25. Along the east, west and south walls, and on a square of tables in between, 30 brand new, networked Dell computer monitors, arrayed on tables, awaited the angels. In a glass enclosed display cabinet, just inside the front door and to the right, there were various pictures of Carl, and one of Karen and Carl in their matching pink Halloween pig costumes, giving testament to his life.

I have been in Carl's computer lab on many occasions with the angels. Wearing their earphones, manipulating their cursers, enthralled with the interactive color monitors, they are blissfully happy there.

Photo of Learning Center
The Carl Daughters Learning Center

"The Rat"

It was the angels' first trip to the Carl Daughters Learning Center.

As usual, Karen had to prepare the angels. So she sat them down on the carpet at the south end of the computer lab, below a row of six computers, and commenced to explain etiquette and parts of the computer.

"Now, we are going to be very quiet in the computer lab, right?"

The angels: "Yessssssssssss."

"We are going to use our small voices, right?"

The angels: "Yesssssssssssss."

When you sit in these chairs, we do not kick the table, do we?"

The angels: "Noooooooooooooo."

Karen pointed to the monitor and said: "This is called the monitor. It's kind of like a television screen."

Karen pointed to an angel and asked; "What is this called?"

"The monitor," came the reply.

Holding a set of earphones, Karen said: "These are earphones. You will wear these when you work on the computer."

Pointing to another angel, Karen asked: "What are these called?"

"Earphones," the angel correctly replied.

Holding up the mouse, Karen said: "This is called a mouse. You will move it around on the table and click a button on the top of the mouse."

Still holding the mouse, Karen asked: "What is this called?"

"The rat," a girl angel spontaneously replied.

Alone

A few days after the memorial held for Carl on the kindergarten playground, a 1st grade boy angel, who had been with Karen and Carl the previous year, stopped by after school to see Karen.

"Mrs. Brown, where is Mr. Daughters?"

"I believe he is in heaven."

"What's he doing in heaven?"

"Probably flying airplanes and playing dodge ball." (Carl had taught the angels how to play dodge ball).

"Are you ever going to see him again?"

"Yes, he is saving a place for me in heaven."

"Are you going to be all alone in Room 1?"

"No, a new teacher will be there to help me."

"Good. I didn't want you to be alone."

They hugged and the little boy angel alighted from the room.

Karate Karen

On a cloudless day, under an azure April sky, Karen wore a striking outfit in red and black as she patrolled the playground. Her fire-engine red, v-neck blouse, with three-quarter length sleeves, flared just above her hips, cinched at the waist by a built-in black sash, perfectly matched her long black pants.

Thus attired, a boy from the kindergarten next door, Room 4, walked up to Karen.

"Mrs. Brown, do you know karate?"

"No," Karen replied.

"Then why are you wearing karate clothes?"

"Karate Karen"

Hoot

Every spring, the arrival of Hoot, the great horned owl, culminated Karen's two-week-long owl unit.

Karen's fascination with owls began when she was 12 years old and attended an arts and crafts fair in Newport Beach. There she encountered a woman in the process of painting a picture of an owl. As Karen and others watched, the painter talked about owls and their amazing physical abilities.

Karen thought owls were such beautiful birds, that day she bought her first owl statue for $1.00. She still has that owl and 1,500 others that she has collected since then. A few hundred are displayed in lighted glass cases in our living room. Many of the owls were gifts over the years, as others learned of Karen's love of owls. I continue to be amazed, that if I point to any owl in Karen's collection, she can tell me how she acquired the owl.

Karen began the owl unit by asking the angels what they knew of owls. Usually, the angels could only name about three properties: It's a bird. It flies. It has wings.

Karen's owl unit, like all of her themed classroom events, was a full court press. Posters of different kinds of owls adorned the walls. A dozen owl books that Karen would eventually read to the angels stood upright along the shelf above the cubbies. Every center activity involved owls: coloring, cutting and pasting owls at the red and yellow centers; listening to owl books at the orange center; reading about owls at the green center; and owl themed math lessons at the blue center. The day before Hoot arrived, the angels made owl headbands and owl wings out of paper sacks.

By the time Hoot arrived, the angels could name over 100 facts about owls, such as: There are over 100 species of owls. Owls primarily eat rodents. Some of the largest owls, eagle owls, can capture small game. Some owls eat mostly fish. An owl's facial feathers form a disc. The disc helps funnel sound to an owl's sensitive ears. Owls can move their facial disks back and forth slightly to help funnel sounds to their ears. Owl's ears are huge cavities in the skull hidden by feathers. Owls can hear a mouse stepping on a twig 75 feet away. A snowy owl can hear a mouse 6" below the snow from 75 feet away. Owls' huge eyes take in the low light at night, when owls hunt. An owl's eyes do not move. The owl's head must move to change the position of the eyes. An owl's neck is so flexible that with the rest of its body motionless, an owl can turn its head to the right so far that it can look over its left shoulder and turn its head so far to the left it can look over its right shoulder. The feathers on an owls' wings have soft edges, so when an owl flies, it makes no sound. Owls swallow their prey whole. The undigested parts are expelled in pellets that fall to the ground. Female owls are larger that male owls. Owl chicks in the nest start trying to fly at three months of age. At six months, they are fully-grown, have flown from the nest, and are on their own.

Before Hoot could fly, he had fallen from his nest in Morro Bay and was rescued by a group that restores injured birds to health to release them back into the wild. Hoot was assigned to Piper Hunter, who had much experience with birds. Piper nursed Hoot back to health. When Hoot was full grown, Piper released Hoot, but he came back to Piper's home. This happened two more times. Hoot kept coming back. Piper thought that maybe Hoot did not know how to hunt, because she had always provided Hoot with mice to eat. So, Piper kept Hoot and started taking Hoot to grade school classrooms. Karen heard about Piper, called her, and Hoot came to Room 1 every year for 15 years.

Karen prepared the angels for Hoot's visit.

"Now we are going to sit way back on the carpet to give Hoot lots of room, aren't we?"

"Yesssssssssss," said the angels. Some angels said "yes" in the sign language that Karen had taught them.

"We are not going to talk when Hoot is here, because we do not want to scare him, do we?"

"Noooooooooo," said the angels. Some angels gestured "no" in the sign language that Karen had taught them.

"Keep sitting criss-cross applesauce, with your hands in your laps, because we do not want to frighten Hoot, do we?"

"Noooooooo," said the angels.

Karen then solicited a number of questions to be asked of Piper and wrote them on the white board.

When Piper entered the classroom, she carried Hoot in a large, gray, plastic pet carrier. The angels sat in rows well back from the Karen's chair at the front of the room. Piper sat in Karen's chair. She put onto her left forearm a large tan leather glove that reached past her elbow. Then she reached down, opened the pet carrier door and Hoot flew up onto her gloved arm, anchored by his powerful four pronged talons. The angels gasped. Hoot was huge. His golden yellow eyes were enormous. Hoot looked down at the angels, who were riveted by his unblinking stare.

In 2009, when Hoot came to Room 1, Piper told the class that Hoot had accidentally escaped and she had just found him outside a local Wal-Mart store. He had flown into a window. [31]

Piper started talking about Hoot and about owls, repeating some of the 100 facts the angels already knew.

---

[31]   In 2010, Piper told Karen that she had loaned Hoot to an experienced bird person and Hoot had accidentally escaped. Hoot was gone for good. His last visit was to Karen's class was in 2009.

Hoot turned his head from side to side as she spoke. Piper spoke for about five minutes.

Then Karen said: "We have some questions for you." Karen then asked the pre-selected questions. Piper answered them.

Then it was time for the finale. Piper lifted her gloved arm up and down as Hoot extended his wings to their five-foot span to maintain his balance. His wings made no sound. Piper lifted Hoot up again and as he flapped his silent wings and in a low voice he said: "Hooo . . . Hooo."

Hoot the Great Horned Owl and his savior,
Piper Hunter

A Secret

A little boy angel in Karen's class walked up to Karen while she was outside on the playground.

He said: "Mrs. Brown, I've got a secret. Can I tell you?"

Karen said: "Well, secrets are meant to be kept."

"But I want to tell you," he continued.

"Well, okay then," said Karen.

"Sometimes my dad dresses in my mom's bra and panties," he said.

"Well honey, thanks for that, but you really need to keep that secret to yourself."

A Missing Slip

A little girl angel came to class and proudly said to Karen: "Mrs. Brown, I'm wearing a slip." So she pulled up her dress to show Karen the slip.

"That's a very nice slip," said Karen.

Later in the morning, the little angel went to use the girls' bathroom. After an interval, the little girl angel came out looking distressed. "Mrs. Brown, I've lost my slip!"

"Well, let's take a look," said Karen. She walked over to the angel, lifted up her dress and found that the angel had tucked the slip into her underpants.

"Here it is," said Karen, as she helped the angel collect her slip and rearrange her clothing.

"Fruck"

Bobby (not his real name) transferred mid-year from Alabama into Karen's kindergarten class.

Bobby's father was in the U.S. Air Force. He had been transferred to Vandenberg Air Force Base in Lompoc, California, about 40 miles south of Grover Beach. Since no on-base housing was then available, the family found a temporary place in Grover Beach, until a spot opened on base.

Karen only had Bobby in her class for a few months. He was handsome, uncommonly kind, and charmed everyone with a beguiling southern drawl. But as Karen was about to discover, he also had some very challenging speech problems.

The first day Bobby joined Karen and her reading group at the green center, Karen began talking about names. Karen asked the angels the names of their parents. Taking turns around the circle, the angels started by stating the names of their fathers.

When Karen got to Bobby, has said: "Mah daddy's name is Fruck."

Karen, a little obtuse, said: "Fruck . . . that's a funny name. I've never heard that name before."

"Y'all know . . . Fruck, as in Farls," Bobby explained.

Getting no response, Bobby continued: "Mah daddy's name is Farls, but they call him Fruck."

Then it dawned on Karen, "Chuck" as in "Charles".

An Autistic Boy Succeeds

A meeting was held prior to placing an autistic boy named Alan, not his real name, into the Karen's class, initially on a part-time basis. Educators call this "mainstreaming." Alan was primarily enrolled in the disabled kindergarten class in Room 7, not far from Room 1.

Alan was blessed with a wonderful mother, who passionately cared for and advocated for him. In the placement meeting, Alan's mother told Karen: "He won't eat the snacks at snack time, because he has food sensitivities.[32] He won't touch anybody and won't want to be touched."

Alan's mother was standing in the back of the classroom on Alan's first day. When snack time rolled around, he stood, selected a snack from the offerings, and ate it. Karen looked back at Alan's mother. Both women were thrilled.

That week, Alan observed the rhythms and routines of the classroom, especially show and tell. The following week it was Alan's first turn to show and tell. He came forward carrying his brown paper bag and stood on Karen's right side, as she sat on her chair facing the angels on the rug. As Alan started to give his clues, he leaned against Karen.

---

[32] An example of a food texture issue for a child on the autism spectrum, would be one who cannot tolerate eating a fresh, raw apple, but can easily eat applesauce.

318

Soon he sat down on her lap as the angels tried to guess what was in his bag.

Karen glanced at Alan's mother in the back of the room. They shared a joyful moment.

After the object had been identified and he had asked for and received three comments, he got up from Karen's lap, put his brown bag into his cubby, and resumed his place on the rug.

Initially, Alan spent two hours per day in Room 1. He progressed so rapidly that soon he was moved into Room 1 full time.

Karen had a remarkable ability to touch the angels' hearts so that they felt totally accepted. That is why angels like Alan were always placed in Room 1 to be welcomed and transformed by Karen.

Body Parts

Karen gave an introductory lesson about body parts: head, eyes, ears, neck, torso, arms, hands, fingers, legs, feet, toes, etc.

The second lesson required the angels to identify parts of the body that were paired. The angels successfully identified: eyes, ears, arms, legs, and feet.

Then Karen asked the angels to identify body parts that numbered more than three. The angels identified: hair, eyelashes, teeth, fingers, and toes.

Karen then held up her hands, saying: "Look at my hands and see if you can figure out something that we have more than one of besides fingers."

An angel proudly answered: "I know. It's wrinkles."

Counting To 65

On the first full day of class in Karen's final academic year, 2010 to 2011, I monitored the red center table from 9:00-9:30 a.m. I had folded my 6'4" frame into a kindergarten chair just 10" off the floor, with the usual result. With my knees on both sides of my shoulders, I resembled a grasshopper at rest.

The angels cut, colored and pasted a gingerbread man.

At the end of the second center, there were a few minutes to spare. On my left sat two boy angels. On my right sat two girl angels. I filled the time by asking my favorite first question.

"How old are you?" I asked the assembled.

Both boys answered: "Five."

Brianna said: "Five." Her elegant long-necked, ivory complexion, dark eyes and close-cropped hair, made me think of a five-year-old Audrey Hepburn.

Cierra assertively answered: "Five and a half." Her powder blue eyes blazed from a porcelain complexion, framed by white blond hair cascading to her waist. I imagined Gwyneth Paltrow at age five "and a half."

I had asked the age question literally scores of times over the previous two years, but no one had ever inquired of me.

321

The precocious Cierra then asked: "How old are you?"

Suspecting I would solicit some charming answers, I asked: "What do you think?"

The boys were stumped into silence.

Brianna hazarded a guess: "Eighteen?"

"No, older than that," I answered.

Cierra took over. "Twenty?"

"No, older than that," I replied.

Cierra eyed me, pondering her next question. Leaning forward in her chair, in a higher tone of voice, she asked: "Forty?"

"No, older than that," I answered.

Leaning fully forward, now nearly parallel to the surface of the table, Cierra squinted, her upward gaze lingering on my full head of gray hair. After an interval she squeezed out, in a high-pitched voice, one final guess: "Seventy?"

"Younger than that. I am 65."

Rolling her eyes to the heavens, Brianna exclaimed: "I can't even COUNT that high."

November

By the end of October, the angels had frequently been exposed to the phrase "say no to drugs" as part of the DARE (Drug Abuse Resistance Education) program.

On the last day of October, at calendar time, Karen prepared to turn over to the new calendar month: November.

"There is a new month after October and it begins with the letter 'N.' Does anybody know what it is called?" she asked.

In unison, the angels responded: "No-drugs."

Music

Room 1 resounded with music, carrying on a tradition dating back to the Greeks.

The ancients mused that music was the most perfect of the arts, for one could understand and appreciate music without the acquisition of special skills in mathematics, the sciences or language. Music was intuitive to man.

Aristotle included instruction in music at the Lyceum. "In general, the ones that are customary to teach are four: letters, gymnastics, music, and a fourth, in some cases, drawing."[33] He further added: "(Musaeus, at any rate says, 'singing is most pleasant for mortals,' and that is why it is with good reason that people accept it into social gatherings and leisure time, because of its power to delight"[34]). Even in the Dark Ages, music was preserved as one of the liberal arts, "because its object was the harmony of the human body."[35]

Karen began every day by placing a 33-1/3 RPM record onto her old black record player to the play "*Good*

---

[33] Aristotle, *Politics, Books VII and VIII*, Translated with a commentary by Richard Kraut, p. 36-37, Oxford University Press (1997).

[34] ID. p. 42.

[35] Barbara W. Tuchman, *A Distant Mirror, The Calamitous 14th Century*, p. 61, Alfred A. Knopf (1978).

Morning"[36]and led the angels as they sat on the carpet and sang. Here is the *"Good Morning"* song.

GOOD MORNING   Words and Music by Bill Fletcher

The "Good Morning" Song

At the end of the day, Karen and the angels sang the *"Goodbye Song"*, to the tune of *"Goodnight Ladies"*. The angels sat on the carpet and sang as Karen faced the angels, sitting in her chair and sometimes standing, accentuating each syllable with gestures:

"Good-bye boys."

---

[36]   Bill Fletcher, *Good Morning, We All Live Together, Vol. 2, p. 5* Youngheart Music Education Service (1978).

(Karen waived her right hand, palm facing outward, across her body from her left to her right, like a windshield wiper)

"Good-bye girls."
(Karen waived her left hand, palm facing outward, across her body from right to left, like a windshield wiper)

"Good-bye everyone."
(Karen pointed at the angels with her right index finger, then her left index finger, alternating with each syllable)

"It's time for us to go."
(Pointing alternate fingers, same as just above)

"I will see you tomorrow, tomorrow, tomorrow."
(Pointing alternate fingers, same as just above)

"I will see you tomorrow."
(Pointing alternate fingers, same as just above)

". . . and I love you this much!"
(Karen, both palms turned towards her face, brought the fingertips of both hands together to her lips and blew a kiss to the angels by extending both hands out in an arc as wide as possible).

Karen got the idea for this song from a fellow teacher, Debbie Highfield.

After recess and just before lunch, Karen used a number of songs to "get the wiggles out," as she would say.

One of the angels' favorites was *"The Freeze."*[37] Played from her old black 33-1/3 RMP record player, the angels all stood and Karen led them as they formed a circle and danced around on the carpet, freezing in place when the music stopped and the voice on the record said: "Freeze."

"The Freeze"

---

[37] *The Freeze*, words and music by *Greg Scelsa, We All Live Together*, Volume 2, p.23, Youngheart Music Education Service (1978).

Hap Palmer was a prolific writer of children's songs. Two of his best were movement songs that Karen frequently used: "*Turn-A-Round*"[38] and "*Opposite*"[39]

In the "*Turn Around*" song, the singer on the record instructed the angels to "turn around" in place, with every refrain.

In the "*Opposite*" song, the angels would be told, for example, to "put your hands high, now do the opposite."[40]

Another one the angels loved was to march around in a circle while listening to "*Looking For Dracula*,"[41] where during the search the angels encounter a "spooky swamp"; a "huge snake"; a "haunted house" and a "great big foot".[42]

Another movement song that convulsed the angels was: "*Head And Shoulders Knees And Toes.*"

With both hands, Karen touched the relevant body part as she pronounced it: head, then shoulders, then knees, and then toes. After about the third chorus, Karen rapidly sped

---

[38] Hap Palmer, *Turn-A-Round, Getting To Know Myself,* Activity Records, Inc.(1972).

[39] Hap Palmer, *Opposite, Getting To Know Myself,* Activity Records, Inc. (1972).

[40] ID

[41] Traditional "Lion Hunt" adapted by Charlotte Diamond, CAPAC, *Looking For Dracula,* 10 Carrot Diamond, Hug Bug Records(1985).

[42] ID

up the rhythm, so that nobody could keep up, and the angels collapsed in laughter.

Besides the movement songs, Karen used a wealth of patriotic songs: *"You're a Grand Old Flag"*; *"God Bless America"*; *"This Land Is Your Land"*; *"Yankee Doodle"*; *"America"*; *"America, The Beautiful"*; *"Battle Hymn Of The Republic"*; *"Columbia The Gem Of The Ocean"*; and *"The Star Spangle Banner"*.

Mr. P. Mooney's happy song enchanted the angels every fall.

The angels' favorite Christmas songs were*: "Rudolph The Red-Nosed Reindeer" and "Jingle Bells"*.

Karen used uplifting Disney Songs*: "Heigh-Ho"; "When You Wish Upon A Star"; "Winnie The Pooh," and "Supercalifr agilisticexpialidocious."*[43]

In the spring, Karen taught the angels the classic old nursery rhyme songs: *"Mary Had A Little Lamb"*; *"Little Boy Blue"*; *"London Bridge"*; *"Old King Cole"*; *"Sing A Song Of Sixpence"*; *"Little Bo Peep"*; *"Mary, Mary, Quiet Contrary"*; *"Humpty Dumpty"*; *"Little Jack Horner"*; *"Jack And Jill"*; *"Hickory, Dickory, Dock"*; *"Baa, Baa, Black Sheep"*; *"Here We Go Round The Mulberry Bush"*; *"Looby-Loo"*; *"A Hunting We Will Go"*; *"Little Jack Horner"*; *"Rock-A-Bye Baby"*; *"Oh*

---

[43]   Walt Disney's Happiest Songs, Walt Disney Music Company (1968).

Where, Oh Where, Has My Little Dog Gone"; "A Hunting We Will Go"; "Twinkle, Twinkle, Little Star"; and "Old MacDonald".

Then there were the miscellaneous songs: "Five Little Monkeys Sitting On A Bed"; "The ABC Song"; "The Days Of The Week"; "The Alphabet"; "If You're Happy And You Know It"; "She'll Be Coming Round The Mountain"; "Michael, Row Your Boat Ashore"; "Paw Paw Patch"; "Billy Boy"; "It's A Small World"; "Bingo"; "Dreydl"; "Six Little Ducks"; "Little White Duck"; "This Old Man"; "Polly Put A Kettle On"; "Farmer In The Dell"; "Ten Little Indians"; "Where Is Thumbkin"; "Skip To My Lou"; "Are You Sleeping"; "I'm A Little Teapot"; "This Old Man"; "On Top Of Old Smoky"; "On Top of My Pizza"; "One Potato"; "Pat-A-Cake"; "Pease Porridg, the "Hukilau"; and "Happy Birthday".

Karen carried the above-described catalogue of songs in her head and would sing any one of them at any appropriate time.

Karen often relied on the prolific Hap Palmer for supplemental melodies that she would play on her 33-1/3 RPM record player.

To calm the angels: "Savannah", "Sea Gulls", "Noonie's Lullaby", "Summer Rain" and "Misty Canyon", from Hap Palmer's Music For Rest And Relaxation.[44]

---

[44]   Hap Palmer, *Sea Gulls… Music For Rest And Relaxation*, Activity Records, Inc. (1978).

For oral language development: *"Witches Brew"*; *"Grandma's Farm"*; *"Scamper"*; *"Clickity Clack"*; *"Goodnight"*; *"Pack Up The Sleigh"*; and *"They Go Together"*.[45]

For music and movement with sticks: *"Make A Pretty Sound"*; *"Knocking On The Door"*; *"Bring Your Sticks"*; *"Homemade Band"*; *"Beautiful Day"*; and *"Stick Dance"*.[46]

For learning basic skills: *"Colors"*; *"Put Your hands Up In The Air"*; *"The Elephant"*; *"The Number March"*; *"Marching Around The Alphabet"*; *"Growing"*; *"This Is The Way We Get Up In The Morning"*; *"The Birds"*; *"What Are You Wearing?"*; and *"What Is Your Name"*.[47]

To excite the angels' sense of imagination: *"Rag Doll"*; *"Guitar Player"*; *"The Friendly Giant"*; *"Rushing"*; *"The Clown"*; *"Little Ants"*; *"Motorcycle Racer"*; *"Kite Song"*; *"Little Elf"*; *"Big Heavy Box"*; *"Jumping Frog"*; and *"The Bullfight"*.[48]

To help with introducing elemental math: *"Marching Around The Number Wheel"*; *"Do You Know"*; *"Adding Sets"*; *"Jumping"*; *"Classic Rock"*; *"Bossa Nova to Eight"*; and *"Answers To Nine"*.[49]

---

[45] Hap and Martha, Palmer, *Witches Brew*, Activity Records, Inc. (1976).

[46] Hap Palmer, *Homemade Band*, Activity Records, Inc.(

[47] Hap Palmer, *Learning Basic Skills Through Music*, Activity Records, Inc. (1969).

[48] Hap Palmer, *Pretend*, Activity Records, Inc. (1975).

[49] Hap Palmer, *Math Readiness Addition And Subtraction*, Activity Records, Inc.(1972).

To help with basic living skills: *"Safety Songs"; "Listen And Do"; "High And Low"; "How Are We Going"; "All On The Table Before You"; "Kinds Of Food"; "Under the Stick"; "Hello"; "Show Me and Walk Under The Circle".*[50] For health and safety: *"Brush Away"; "Stop, Look and Listen"; and "Buckle Your Seat Belt".*[51]

Finally, Karen played songs just for fun: *"Do A Little Dance"; "Clap And Rest"; "Slow And Fast"; "Soft And Loud"; "¾ rag"; "Scales"; "Joy"; "Walking Notes"; "Together"; "Five Beats Of Each Measure"; "Good Old-fashioned Rock And Roll Song"; "Touch The World and Quickly And Quietly".*[52]

There is no more beautiful sound in all the world than that of the voices of children raised in song.

---

[50] Hap Palmer, *Learning Basic Skills Through Music (Vocabulary)*, Activity Records, Inc. (1969).

[51] ID.

[52] Hap Palmer, *The Feel Of Music*, Activity Records, Inc. (1974).

Pedegogy[53]

The day after Labor Day in 1950, dawned sunny and warm in Omaha, Nebraska as my mother, Mary, took me by the hand and walked me three blocks to the Henry W. Yates Elementary School and into Mrs. Howard's kindergarten. The room seemed enormous, with a high ceiling, and a wall of south-facing windows that bathed the room on a sunny day with nearly blinding ambient light, further reflected off of the polished oak floor. I remember: how Mrs. Howard was so sweet and kind; brief naps on a small rug, which I had brought from home; snacks of milk and cookies; playing a triangle while marching in a circle; playtime on the playground; and singing songs.

After grade school, high school, college, graduate school, and law school, kindergarten was the most fun I ever had at school.

Little was expected of me in kindergarten. Only in 1st grade did reading and language instruction officially begin. It was in 1st grade that I encountered an "adoption", a reading program that I remember as "Dick and Jane." It contained such electric sentences as: "Dick."; "Jane."; "See Dick." and "See Jane." It was boring beyond belief. To this day, I

---

[53] "The art or science of teaching; especially instruction in teaching methods." *Webster's New World Dictionary of the American Language, College Edition*, p. 1077, Id B. Guralnik & Joseph H. Friend General Editors, The World Publishing Company (1966).

resent it. I had already been reading books before I came to kindergarten. My mother, a gifted teacher, who was prodigiously well read, made sure my (brilliant) sister, Cheri, and I were reading at an early age. I was raised in a home bursting with books. Happiness for me is to be alone with a well-written book.

A word about textbook "adoptions." Karen tells me that approximately every seven years in California, the state educational leaders give teachers a list of approximately three publishers, educators call this the "state matrix", from which to choose their new textbooks (whether they need them or not).

One teacher from each school comprises a "district committee." The district committee arranges to have teachers select one of the textbooks to "pilot" (try to use them) in their classrooms for a period. Each grade pilots each of the three textbooks. Then the district committee selects the winning textbook company.

As I would say in a pleading, I am informed, believe, and thereon allege that the system of "adoptions", at least as applied to kindergarten, is a colossal waste of money.

When I think of the adoption of the insipid "Dick and Jane" that I endured in 1951, I now wonder, was *McGuffey's First Eclectic Reader* suddenly too difficult? It had been in use since 1837, and continued to be used somewhere in America until the late 1970's. It's phonic chart listed: "Long

Vocals; Short Vocals; Diphthongs; Aspirates; Subvocals and Substitutes."[54]

Yet when I was taught phonics in 1st grade, in 1951, I was taught that each vowel had only a short and long, sound. During Karen's career, she initially taught only the short sound of each vowel. By February each year, she introduced the long vowel sounds, occurring after a silent "e"; as in "rat" and "rate," and "cap" and "cape."

In Karen's first 10 years teaching kindergarten, the angels were only expected to know the names of the upper and lower case letters, and to be able to recognize numbers 1-10. Educators call these "outcomes." The teaching of phonics was not required, and no reading was expected. (Karen taught phonics anyway and commencing with her tenure at Grover City Elementary and the spectacular Hawaii English Project[55] had her kids reading small books and recognizing numbers 1-30). Gradually, what had for eons been 1st grade curricula got pushed down into kindergarten. Thus the kindergarten "outcomes" became: identification of all capital and lower case letters, vowel sounds, ten sight words, word recognition, and the reading of simple, small books.

Karen never bored an angel or wasted an angel's time by slavish adherence to an "adopted" reading or language

---

[54] William H. McGuffey, *McGuffey's First Eclectic Reader, Revised Edition*, p. 96-97, Van Nostrand Reinhold Company (1879).

[55] *Hawaii English Project*, Hawaii Department of Education (1970).

program. She individualized the instruction and urged each angel along according to his or her current ability.

Karen took the best of any adoption, discarded the useless parts, and by this eclectic approach, became a master teacher. Mr. P. Mooney[56] and the geometric Try Task[57] shapes had been abandoned in storage in Room 1, when Karen arrived in 1976. She used them for the next 35 years. The Hawaii English Project was soon discarded. She rescued the materials before they were destroyed and used them for 29 more years. After the Wright Group[58] materials were discarded, she kept them and used parts of them for another 20 years. After she found Zoo-phonics, she used it for the remainder of her career, replacing the generic phonics she had been teaching. Karen always served on the committees that investigated and piloted the new proposed adoptions, but the adoptions were seldom better than what she had been using, and some were virtually useless. Karen indicates that publishers don't devote much attention to kindergarten, because kindergarten is not mandatory in California, and probably many other states and thus, the market is smaller.

---

[56] *Peabody Language Development Kits-Revised*, senior author Lloyd M. Dunn, American Guidance Service (1981). NB. This is the updated version.

[57] *Try Task*, California Sate Series, California State Department of Education. Noble and Noble (1967).

[58] *The Wright Group Publishing, Inc. (1995).*

Karen's methods addressed each angel's needs, individually. She did this by grouping the angels. This started in May at Kindergarten Roundup, where Karen got to meet and assess many of the angels as they enrolled for next fall's classes. By the end of the third day of kindergarten in Room 1, Karen had grouped all the angels, according to their then current knowledge of colors, shapes, letters, and numbers.

In the first full week, Karen taught the angels how to use her color-coded center system.

Karen's self-designed, color-coded system arranged up to 32 angels into four groups, from the most advanced to the least advanced. Karen created this system several days before she began teaching her first kindergarten class at Branch School.

Each angel would check the color-coded chart just inside the front door, to learn which two centers to go to on Monday, Tuesday, Wednesday and Thursday. Each day, Monday through Thursday, Karen hung a different vertical strip next to the angels' names, showing which two colored centers the angels went to that day. The first center occurred from 9:00 a.m. to 9:15 a.m. The angels went to their second center from 9:15 a.m. to 9:30 a.m. This was double duty, as some kindergarten teachers used only one center task per day.

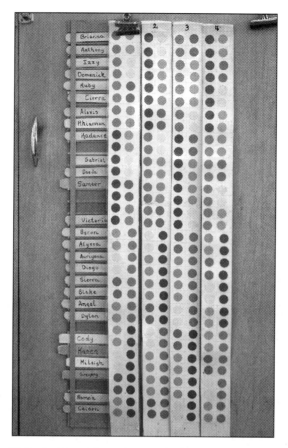

FIG. 1: Karen's color-coded center system

Under this well-organized system, once per week, each angel attended: the **red** center and the **yellow** center for small motor development to complete coloring, cutting, tracing, and pasting tasks, sometimes involving food preparation, like buttering a slice of bread; the **orange** center to listen to books on tape; the **pink** center to work on Try Task shapes and handwriting, learning in the process to track from left to right and top to bottom; and twice per week to the **green** reading/language center with Karen, and to the **blue** math center with an part-time teacher.

Under this system, stereotyping was minimized. Each day, the angels would appear at one center with their ability group, then at the second center with angels from every ability group.

Every piece of paper produced by the angels at the centers, all supporting the theme for the month (i.e., Gingerbread Man, Brown Bear, etc.), was immediately displayed on the classroom walls, and taken down and taken home at the end of the theme for the month.

Karen placed into every cubbie at the start of the year, a laminated rectangle upon which she had printed, in black marker, the angel's first name. From the first day of the first full week, Karen daily directed the angels, using their Ticonderoga Beginners pencils, to write their first names. Those initial efforts were energetic, and charmingly erratic, but Karen had the angels writing their first names so often that practice did soon make perfect. In the spring, Karen added a second laminated signature strip, containing the angel's last name. It was remarkable, over time, to see the signatures develop a dramatic clarity, as the angels developed their small motor skills to write their own names. They did so with well-earned pride.

Also starting in the first full week of school, Karen introduced the sounds of the letters of the alphabet. On Monday, Karen introduced ABC. On Tuesday, she reviewed ABC and introduced new letters: DEF. On Wednesday, Karen reviewed ABC, DEF and then introduced new letters:

GHI. On Thursday and Friday, the nine letters that had been introduced that week were reviewed. Karen repeated the process, as the level of the class permitted, until she had introduced the entire alphabet. This process usually took six weeks. Only after the class had been introduced to the 26 letters of the alphabet did Karen introduce the sounds made by the letters via Zoo-phonics.

The value of Zoo-phonics was the manner in which it provided triple reinforcement in learning the alphabet. First, the rhyme of "allie alligator says ah ah", helped the angels hear and remember the sound of the letter "a". Second, the use of a colorful drawing of an alligator wrapped around an "a", helped the angels see and remember the letter "a". Third, the kinetic gesture of extending both arms forward, one on top of the other, then closing them together with each "ah . . . ah', like an alligator biting down, further helped the angels remember the letter "a."

Figure 2 shows the three-page Zoo-phonics[59] hand out Karen provided to the parents on Back To School Night.

---

[59]   Zoo-phonics, Inc. 1999.

Zoo-phonics Signals

Watch the video. Have your children watch it. It can be a centers activity.

girl

a — **alligator (allie alligator):** Extend arms forward, one over the other, to form an alligator's mouth. Open and close the hands and arms, and say the short sound for "a." Sustain sound.

boy

b — **bear (bubba bear):** Reach your dominant hand above your head to an imaginary honey hive. Bring the honey to your mouth in a fist, as a bear might do, but don't touch your mouth, and say the *sound* of the letter "b."

girl

c — **cat (catina cat):** Pretend you are a cat washing your face with a paw. Say the *sound* of the letter "c."

girl

d — **deer (deedee deer):** Use two fingers of each hand to form deer ears on the sides of your head. Say the *sound* of the letter "d."

girl

e — **elephant (ellie elephant):** Take one arm and swing the hand up to your mouth, as if Ellie were feeding herself a peanut, hay or water. Say the short sound for "e." Sustain sound.

girl

f — **fish (francy fish):** With your hands (palms down) in front of your chest, place the palm of one hand on the back of the other hand to form a fish, and then wiggle your thumbs. Make sure you have a thumb on each side. Say the sound of the letter "f." Sustain sound.

boy

g — **gorilla (gordo gorilla):** Pretend you are peeling a banana, and say the sound of the letter "g."

girl

h — **horse (honey horse):** Slap both sides of your thighs or hips, suggesting a horse galloping. Say the sound of the letter "h."

Fig. 2: Zoo-phonics signals: "a to h".

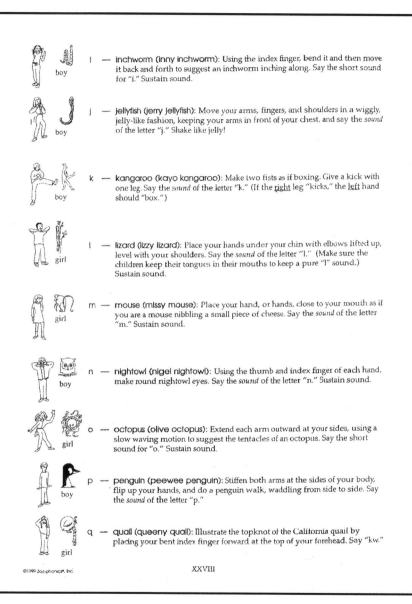

i — **inchworm (inny inchworm):** Using the index finger, bend it and then move it back and forth to suggest an inchworm inching along. Say the short sound for "i." Sustain sound.

boy

j — **jellyfish (jerry jellyfish):** Move your arms, fingers, and shoulders in a wiggly, jelly-like fashion, keeping your arms in front of your chest, and say the *sound* of the letter "j." Shake like jelly!

boy

k — **kangaroo (kayo kangaroo):** Make two fists as if boxing. Give a kick with one leg. Say the *sound* of the letter "k." (If the right leg "kicks," the left hand should "box.")

boy

l — **lizard (lizzy lizard):** Place your hands under your chin with elbows lifted up, level with your shoulders. Say the *sound* of the letter "l." (Make sure the children keep their tongues in their mouths to keep a pure "l" sound.) Sustain sound.

girl

m — **mouse (missy mouse):** Place your hand, or hands, close to your mouth as if you are a mouse nibbling a small piece of cheese. Say the *sound* of the letter "m." Sustain sound.

girl

n — **nightowl (nigel nightowl):** Using the thumb and index finger of each hand, make round nightowl eyes. Say the *sound* of the letter "n." Sustain sound.

boy

o — **octopus (olive octopus):** Extend each arm outward at your sides, using a slow waving motion to suggest the tentacles of an octopus. Say the short sound for "o." Sustain sound.

girl

p — **penguin (peewee penguin):** Stiffen both arms at the sides of your body, flip up your hands, and do a penguin walk, waddling from side to side. Say the *sound* of the letter "p."

boy

q — **quail (queeny quail):** Illustrate the topknot of the California quail by placing your bent index finger forward at the top of your forehead. Say "kw."

girl

XXVIII

Fig.2: Zoo-phonics signals: "i to q"

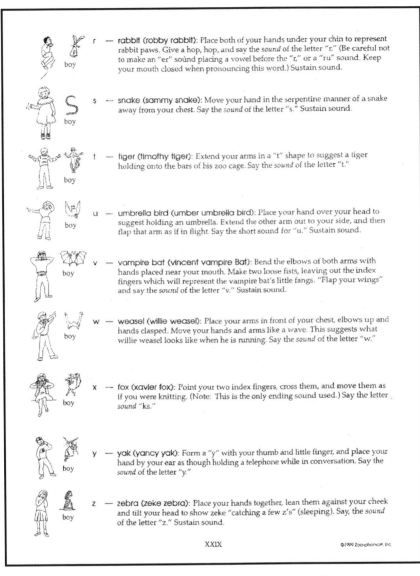

r — rabbit (robby rabbit): Place both of your hands under your chin to represent rabbit paws. Give a hop, hop, and say the *sound* of the letter "r." (Be careful not to make an "er" sound placing a vowel before the "r," or a "ru" sound. Keep your mouth closed when pronouncing this word.) Sustain sound.

s — snake (sammy snake): Move your hand in the serpentine manner of a snake away from your chest. Say the *sound* of the letter "s." Sustain sound.

t — tiger (timothy tiger): Extend your arms in a "t" shape to suggest a tiger holding onto the bars of his zoo cage. Say the *sound* of the letter "t."

u — umbrella bird (umber umbrella bird): Place your hand over your head to suggest holding an umbrella. Extend the other arm out to your side, and then flap that arm as if in flight. Say the short sound for "u." Sustain sound.

v — vampire bat (vincent vampire Bat): Bend the elbows of both arms with hands placed near your mouth. Make two loose fists, leaving out the index fingers which will represent the vampire bat's little fangs. "Flap your wings" and say the *sound* of the letter "v." Sustain sound.

w — weasel (willie weasel): Place your arms in front of your chest, elbows up and hands clasped. Move your hands and arms like a wave. This suggests what willie weasel looks like when he is running. Say the *sound* of the letter "w."

x — fox (xavier fox): Point your two index fingers, cross them, and move them as if you were knitting. (Note: This is the only ending sound used.) Say the letter sound "ks."

y — yak (yancy yak): Form a "y" with your thumb and little finger, and place your hand by your ear as though holding a telephone while in conversation. Say the *sound* of the letter "y."

z — zebra (zeke zebra): Place your hands together, lean them against your cheek and tilt your head to show zeke "catching a few z's" (sleeping). Say, the *sound* of the letter "z." Sustain sound.

Fig.2: Zoo-phonics signals: "r to z."

The Hawaii English Project (HEP) was the foundational material. Beginning in the first full week, Karen started introducing the HEP materials. This was done between 10:00 and 10:30 a.m., Monday through Thursday.

The heart of the HEP program consisted of 25 stacks of flip cards. Each stack consisted of up to 285 cards. The cards were double sided, so the "teacher," who sat on one side, could ask the "student," who sat opposite, the proper question and know the correct answer. The side seen by the "teacher" was identical to the reverse side seen by the "student."

By progressing through the flip cards, the angels learned the letters, also numbers to 30 and small words. HEP did not have a phonics component, so Karen taught phonics separately and simultaneously.

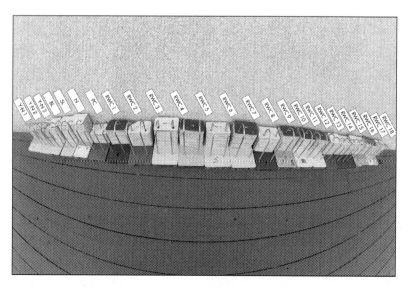

Fig. 3: the HEP stacks

Here is a synopsis of the sections:

The first three sections were designated "Y-N 1"; "Y-N 2" and "Y-N 3".

"Y-N" refers to the words: "Yes" and "No".

"Y-N 1" cards consisted of double-sided flip cards each containing two capital letters. Flipping a card forward, the "tutor" asked the "student": "Are these the same or different?" The correct answer would be either "yes" or "no". Thus the designation: "Y-N 1". The stacks were divided into sections beginning with a blue card, which introduced a new word category, usually followed by up to 10 flip cards. If an angel got the first eight cards right but missed on #9, the tutor was instructed to go back to the beginning blue card and start over. Nobody ever got a pass. This was serious work and the "tutors" and their "students" gave the cards close attention. The "student's" sticky tab with his/her name on it was left in the place where the tutoring stopped for the day. Tutoring resumed again from the position of the sticky tab forwards.

Karen and Irene would first take an advanced angel through "Y-N 1", before that angel would qualify to tutor another angel on Y-N 1.

Karen had a separate short stack of HEP diagnostics that she applied to each angel in the preliminary grouping process.

At the end of each stack the last 20 flip cards constituted a review and testing of the presented materials. If the angel could answer the final review flip cards, the angel checked out, got a much-deserved award, and moved on to the next series.

"Y-N, 2" cards consisted of two small letters, like "b" and "d", on each flip card. The same "yes" or "no" response was solicited.

"Y-N, 3" cards consisted of two one-syllable words, containing the same sounds: "win" and "tin"; "rid" and "rip"; "saw" and "was."

The next stack, "BL" consisted of the "big" or capital letters of the alphabet, one letter per page. The angel needed to correctly identify each letter. Karen thought the review/testing materials at the end of the stack were not detailed enough, so she created her own set of 26 flip cards that tested the entire alphabet, before an angel could pass "BL" and get an award.

The next stack, "SL," displayed all 26 small letters of the alphabet, one letter per page. Like the "BL" stack, the review/ testing materials at the end of the stack were not tough enough for Karen, so she devised her own set of cards, testing on all 26 small letters.

The next stack was designated as "N", consisted of numbers 1-30, one number per page. As with the "BL" and

"SL" stacks, Karen devised her own more strenuous testing materials, testing all 30 numbers.

It should be obvious by now that this system allowed each student to move at his/her own pace. The gifted students could move rapidly and the slowest student could move slowly, each according to her/his own abilities.

It was a real accomplishment to master Y-N, 1,2 & 3 and BL and SL.

The next section was "PC," picture cards. The cards start with the sounds like "s" and "m", then move onto words starting with and "s", like "sat" and with and "m" like "mat," etc. On the back of each card, seen by the "teacher," is a drawing creating a picture described by the word on the opposite side. A floor mat adorns the back of the word "mat."

The next 18 sections are designated "RWC"—Reading Word Card, ranging from "RWC 1" to "RWC 18."

I will generally describe the first eight RWC sections.

"RWC-1" emphasized single-syllable words containing the "at" "an" and "ad." The front or "student," side of the card contained a single word, like: "cat", "rat", "mat", "sat", "hat", "fat", "map", "lap", "sad" and "mad." On the back, or "teacher," side of the card, a picture appeared, describing the word, like the picture of a cat.

"RWC-2" emphasized "ap", "at", "ad" and "ag", with words like "map", "lap", "sad", "mad", "cat", and "bag." Previous words were reviewed.

"RWC-3", presented "it, "in" and "ip"; in words like: "sit", "bit", "tin", "fin", "dip" and "rip." Previous words were also reviewed.

"RWC-4" presented "ig", "id", "ix" and "in"; using words like: "fig", "pig", "hid", "did", "mix", and "fix", plus review words.

"RWC-5" presented "op", "ot", "og" and "ox"; in words like: "box", "fox", "mop", "hop", "cot", "got", "dog" and "hog", plus review words.

"RWC-6" revisited: "an", "in", "ad", "id", and introduced "un", "ut", "ub", "um", "up", "ug" and "ud" in the form of the words: "bun", "sun"; "rut", "but"; "tub", "rub"; "sum", "gum"; "tug", "mug", "sud" and "bud."

"RWC-7" mixed previously presented vowels, and introduced short "e" sounds of "et" and "en", with the words "pet", "vet" and "pen", "men."

"RWC-8" presents "ed", "eg", "en", "et", and adds a plural "s", so that "rag" becomes "rags", and "net" becomes "nets."

Most angels do not get past RWC-8, but several in Karen's 35 years got all the way through to RWC-18.

It is usually December/January before the top group completes RWC-4, and then small books are presented, beginning with *An Apple,* to be followed, as ability allowed, by up to 25 other similar books.

The middle two groups reach RWC-4 in March/April at the latest, and commence reading *An Apple* and other books.

The bottom group, despite extra tutoring from Karen and Irene, seldom ever got to RWC 4. The angels in that group got to RWC-1 and RWC-2, and could do some decoding, but could not be said to have the ability to read. These angels were usually those who started too early, at age four, and some would repeat kindergarten and later thrive. Some were afflicted by conditions like ADD, or ADHD, problems at home, or were just slower functioning

The angels continue to progress through the RWC stacks until the school year ends. It is common for the top group to progress to RWC-12.

The system requires the keeping of careful records. Figure 4 shows an identical sample of Karen master class spreadsheet for all 25 stack sections from "YN1" to "RWC-18"

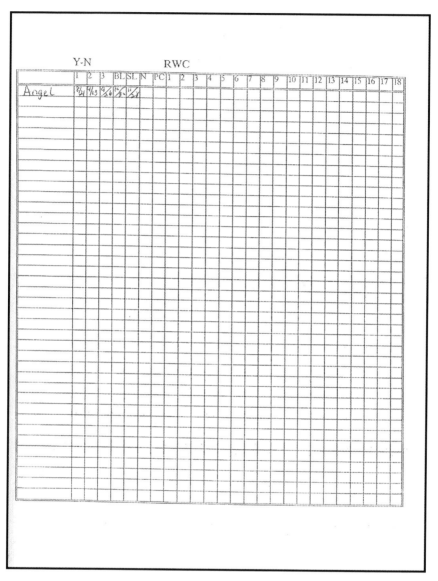

FIG 4: Karen's class spreadsheet for the HEP stacks

Note that in this example, "Angel," a student, has completed the first 5 stacks. He completed YN-1 on August 21st, YN-2 on September 13th, Y-N 3 on September 26th, BL (Big Letters) on October 30th and SL (Small Letters) on November 28th.

How did Karen keep track of all this?

Karen wrote Angel's name onto a clear plastic sticky tab and initially placed it on top of the YN-1 stack. Angel's progress was easily tracked, because his tab was placed in the stack to the point of his progress, at the end of each session, marking his place.

When Karen tested Angel and he passed the test for YN-1, Karen took Angel's sticky tab and affixed it to a corresponding record in his red Records folder, and wrote out a cherished AWARD for Angel, stating that he had completed YN=1 and that date.

Karen then took the sticky tab upon which she had written the date of completion of YN-1 and placed it into Angel's Records folder. Then she created new sticky tab for Angel and placed it at the beginning of the next HEP stack section.

At the start of the school year, Karen provided the angels with three folders. The Homework folder went home on Mondays, and was to be completed and returned on Friday. The Journal folder never went home, until the last day of school. The angels wrote in their journals with Karen at the blue center throughout the school year. The Records folder stayed in the cubbie and was happily brought out to record the completion of a stack series (and for all other elements of the HEP), and to record the receipt of an award.

Angel	Angel	Angel	Angel	Angel
8/21 KB	9/13 KB	9/26 KB	10/30 KB	11/18 KB
YN1	YN2	YN3	BL	SL
N	PC1	RWC1	RWC2	RWC3
RWC4	RWC5	RWC6	RWC7	RWC8
RWC9	RWC10	RWC11	RWC12	RWC13
RWC14	RWC15	RWC16	RWC17	RWC18

PHRASES & SENTENCES

PS6	PS12

AUDIO CARD BOOKS

1	2	3	4	5
6	7	8	9	10
11	12	13	14	15
16	17	18	19	20

Fig 5: Angel's' Records folder sheet to
track progress in HEP stacks

As Figure 5 illustrates, Karen has taken the sticky tab
after Angel passed the review test for YN-1 and placed it
into Angel's Records folder. In so doing, Karen wrote onto

352

the tab the date Angel completed the task. He completed YN-1 on "8/21" and confirmed by Karen's initials, "KB". In this manner, Karen knew exactly where an angel had progressed in learning to read.

The angels cherished their Records folders. They poured over them after getting an award. This folder helped get the angels deeply invested in their own progress towards the ultimate goal of reading books.

I had noticed a flurry of activity every day starting at 10:00 a.m. when Karen formed angels into "teacher" and "student" pairs for the day's HEP activities, based on her groupings and intimate knowledge of each angel's progress through the stacks, and based on her class spreadsheets.

Besides HEP, there were other important elements to Karen's reading program.

As can be seen in Fig 5, there were also sections to keep track of the angel's progress in "Phrases and Sentences"; and in "Audio Card Books." Karen had separate class spreadsheets for same, but I have not displayed them here.

Figure 6 presents another page from the angel's Records book, showing the record sections for "Phonics C"; "Phonics D", "Try Task I" and "Try Task 2" and five typing sections.

PHONICS C

1	2	3	4	5	6	7	8	9
1	2	3	4	5	6	7	8	9

PHONICS D

1	2	3	4	5	6	7	8	9
1	2	3	4	5	6	7	8	9

TRY TASK 1

1	3	5	7	9	11	13	15	17	19	21	23	25	27	29	31
33	35	37	39	41	43	45	47	49	51	53	55	57	59	61	63
65	67	69	71	73	75	77	79	81	83	85	87	89	91	93	95
97	99	101	103	105	107	109	111	113	115	117	119	121	123	125	127

TRY TASK 2

1	3	5	7	9	11	13	15	17	19	21	23	25	27	29	31
33	35	37	39	41	43	45	47	49	51	53	55	57	59	61	63
65	67	69	71	73	75	77	79	81	83	85	87	89	91	93	95

TYPING

DKFJ	SLDK	GFDLSK	GFHASDLJK	RFGK
P.6	P.9	P.13	P.16	P.18

Fig 6: Angel's Records folder sheet to track
progress in Phonics and Try Task

The two top sections of the form, called "Phonics C"
and "Phonics D," referred to box "C" and box "D" of the
Systems 80 machines. Angels had to earn the use of these

pre-computer machines. They had to have mastered their small and capital letters. Once there, they sat in front of one of the four machines. A 33 1/3 rpm record was inserted into the machine. The angel then donned headphones and listened for the narration, which was matched with a visual display. The narrator on the record asked questions, which required the angel to push one of five keys on the keyboard to select a correct answer. Section "C" and "D" each had nine records, double sided.

Karen used the System 80 materials until they were removed from her classroom in about 2008, because the machines broke down and nobody knew how to fix them. I cannot cite a copyright reference, as I no longer have access to the materials.

The bulk of the spaces in Fig 6 allowed the recording of progress in the Try Task geometric shapes puzzles. These tasks were coordinated daily by Irene at the Pink Center. The Try Task materials, identified as the California State Series, published in 1967 by Noble and Noble for the California State Department of Education, were in a cabinet in Room 1 when Karen arrived in 1976. She faithfully used these superb materials for 35 years, because she never found anything to supersede them.

Try Task offered three types of materials. Karen used two. Try Task 1 consisted of hard backed notebooks, containing 127 right-hand pages of geometric shapes formed into horizontal rows, and a tray of red plastic geometric shapes.

(The obsolete typing section referred to a long gone computer keyboard typewriter that Karen and Carl initially had in the classroom, but it broke down about a year after Karen got to Grover Beach and was not replaced).

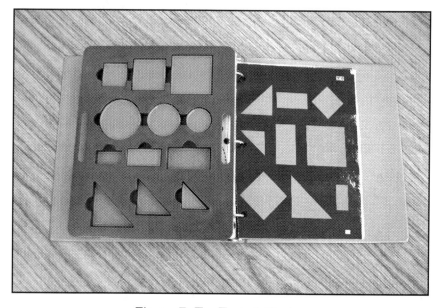

Figure 7: Try Task 1 Binder

Figure 7 is a photograph of a Try Task 1 exercise. The angel placed the tray of geometric shapes on the left side of the binder, and then took from that tray the appropriate shapes to cover the shapes drawn on the right side of the binder, moving from left to right and top to bottom. After Irene had checked for accuracy, the angel removed and replaced the geometric shapes in reverse order.

Try Task 2, consisted of six-sided blocks with different angled lines on each side. The blocks had to be correctly aligned with up to 95 templates. I have not provided a picture of Try Task 2 materials.

Karen had a separate spreadsheet, which I have not displayed here, to keep track of the progress of the entire class with the Try Task 1 and 2 results.

As the angels started reading books, Karen had a separate spreadsheet for the entire class, which I have not displayed here. Each angel had, in his or her Records folder, a sheet entitled "Instructional Library", which recorded the books they had read.

INSTRUCTIONAL LIBRARY

1 An Apple   3-19   kB
2
3
4
5
6
7
8
9
10
11
12
13
14
15
16
17
18
19
20

FIG 8: Angel's' Records folder sheet to track progress in Instructional Library (books).

Figure 8 displays this Records sheet, with a notation that the angel completed the book *An Apple*, on March 15th as initialed by Karen, "KB".

In the angel's Records folder, as displayed in Figure 8, a final page recorded the angel's progress in "Handwriting", "Colors & Shapes", and a comprehensive category entitled: "Plurals, English, Determiners & Dialect Markers." Karen kept track of class progress in each of these categories on separate spreadsheets, which I have elected not to display here.

HANDWRITING

xødg AB :0-19	ces	fbl	thk
iuw	yjr	nmp	qvzx
CGO	SIL	TJU	BKA
BDM	NPR	EFZ	VWXY

COLORS & SHAPES

C	S	C&S

PLURALS, ENGLISH, DETERMINERS & DIALECT MARKERS

PLURALS	E:1-5	E:6-10	E:11-15
E:16-20	E:21-25	E:26-30	E:30-35
DET	DM:1-5	DM:6-10	DM:11-15

Fig. 9: Angel's Records folder sheet to track progress in Handwriting; Colors & Shapes; Plurals; English; Determiners and Dialect Markers

As Figure 9 shows, under the Handwriting section, the first eight boxes contain the 26 small letters of the alphabet and the bottom eight boxes contain the 26 capital letters of the alphabet. This was Karen's invention.

Karen created the small letter groupings according to shapes. The first group, in the upper left-hand corner, isolates the four letters "aodg," as the circular shapes needed to write those letters are so similar.

In order to acquire these writing skills, the angel would be given a sheet of lined paper, with a properly written small "a". The angel would then need to write three full lines below, repeating the correctly written small letter "a".

Once that was accomplished, Irene would draw a vertical line through the letter "a" in the first box. In the example in Figure 9, the angel has completed the entire "aodg" sequence. At that time, the date is written, in this case, "10-15", initialed by Karen and the angel gets an award.

The small center section designated "Colors & Shapes" followed the same pattern. When an angel checked out on all colors and shapes, from a separate set of flip cards, the date was noted, Karen initialed the box, and an award was given.

The bottom single section identified as "Plurals, English, Determiners & Dialect Markers", operated in the same way. The "Plurals" materials were HEP materials on blue flip cards kept near the HEP stacks. The eight boxes concerning English were HEP materials on golden flip cards, stored near the HEP stacks. The Determiners were HEP materials on red flip cards.

Karen's kindergarten operated within the Lucia Mar Unified School District. Several years into her teaching career at Grover City Elementary School, all the kindergartens in the district were tested regarding progress in reading and language. Karen's kindergarten scored the highest. The district then asked Karen how she did it. She noted that she used Mr. P. Mooney and HEP with her own phonics component, so the district bought Mr. P. Mooney sets for everybody.

A few years later, the school district abandoned HEP, which had been used in Grover City and two other grade schools, in favor of a new "adoption." So Karen, with permission, kept a complete set of HEP materials, using them as the foundation of her reading/language program, and with them successfully taught another 900 angels over the next 29 years.

The beauty of the HEP system, and the other eclectic materials used by Karen, was that they: (1) challenged the angels; (2) allowed each angel to progress at his or her own pace; and (3) allowed Karen to track on a daily basis the progress of her students. Unlike other teachers, Karen did not need to periodically test her students to determine their progress in reading and language. She knew where they were at all times.

One of the advantages of the HEP system was the reinforcement that the angels who had already passed that particular stack section, say YN-2, received when they acted as the "tutor" for another angel, who was the "student" trying to master and complete YN-2. When a "student" angel completed YN-2 and passed Karen's test on that stack, the "student" angel got presented with a cherished award presented just before dismissal and got: (1) to leave the rug first to go outside early to get his or her back pack; (2) dismissed first; (3) free choice to play with any toys; and (4) become a "tutor" for another angel who had not yet mastered stack YN-2. The "tutor" who had been tutoring the angel when the award earned was recognized, applauded, and granted the same rights to early first dismissal and free choice toy time.

With this time-tested, eclectic approach, all of Karen's angels who went on to first grade could decode words and almost all were reading small books.

When an angel learned to read, the entire world opened.

The Maestro

Karen was a maestro, commanding the angels' rapt attention, as she conducted them through the symphony of kindergarten. She merely had to raise her hand, or her voice, and all stopped to seek direction from her.[60]

Karen maintained high standards in everything: in class control; in the elaborate themes and themed materials; in the granting of awards; in the top-notch supplies she provided; in the quality of every themed coloring, cutting, tracing and pasting activity; in the manner of class movement from one place on campus to another; in making the angels maintain respectful behavior towards each other; in NEVER allowing bullying, or unkind remarks; in seeing to correct diet in the cafeteria, and on and on and on.

The best lessons plans and the best materials are useless if the teacher cannot control the classroom. Karen once briefly worked with a teacher whose lesson plans were so intricately detailed as to be works of art. Yet when Karen visited that teacher's classroom, it was chaos.

---

[60] In May of her final year, I filmed an entire day of Karen's teaching, from 8:30 in the morning till 1:15 in the afternoon. After I have finished this book, I will get the digital record put onto discs so Karen and I can watch and remember her glorious time among the angels.

The angels were drawn to Karen. They could tell how much she cared about them. Karen was always animated and positive. Karen kept the angels' attention with her smiling expressive face and expressive language, by changing superlatively arranged and organized, attractive activities every 15 minutes, and above all-by setting out clear rules for every activity, and CONSTANTLY ENFORCING the rules in a positive way.

For example, the angels knew that they had to stop Toy Time (which lasted about 15 minutes), when Karen rang the small silver bell on her desk, and then were to quickly replace all the toys. If an angel did not stop, Karen noticed and warned the angel that the next time that happened, he/she would be placed into a time out.

If it happened again, the angel went immediately into time out, Karen remarking: "We don't behave that way in here."

To get out of time out, Karen sat down in a kid chair, level with the angel, and asked: "Why are you here?" If she got an evasive reply, the time out continued. This rarely happened; usually the angel clearly understood what he/she had done wrong and admitted it. Karen again reiterated: "We don't do that (offending behavior) in here."

Rarely did an angel make the same mistake a third time, but if it happened again, then the angel would lose the next Toy Time altogether.

Karen did not directly accuse an angel. She always said: "We don't do that in here."

Any upset Karen had, or had to feign, quickly disappeared, and Karen used the first opportunity, or created an opportunity, usually that same day, to praise the recently offending angel.

I did not naturally come to do this. Once on a first day of school, a discipline problem another teacher could not handle was moved into Karen's class. (This occurred constantly. Karen always got the hard cases, because she could manage to get through to them and everyone knew it). After clearly being told the playground rules, which included the injunction against throwing sand, he threw sand that got into another boy's eye. I wanted him expelled. But Karen used her combination of punishment with positive reinforcement, and soon that boy, who had been such a problem, was thriving in class and behaving on the playground. I continued to be amazed at how Karen could discipline an angel one moment and be praising him or her the next.

Karen never stopped enforcing her rules, and the angels knew it. The first six weeks were the hardest. Often the angel had come from a chaotic home and boundaries were new. Sometimes a lack of parenting skills had allowed an angel to dominate at home.

Karen expended a lot of energy making sure the angels followed her commands, because ultimately, nobody can learn in a chaotic classroom. Furthermore, a chaotic class is not safe.

Karen gradually gave the angels more playground responsibility.

On opening day the playground rules were explained: sit on your bottom on the swings and the slides; only an adult can push you on a swing; no jumping off of any equipment; go across monkey bars with your hands, but don't climb onto the top; no chasing; it is okay to run on the grass, not on the asphalt; don't throw sand; and don't put your hands on anybody.

In the second week Karen introduced balls: rubber balls, basketballs, and a soccer ball. Only the soccer ball could be kicked and only on the grass. If the soccer ball was kicked over the fence, soccer was suspended for the remainder of the play period and the boy who kicked the ball over the fence was given a time out. If the same boy kicked the soccer ball over the fence in a future recess period, he was suspended from soccer for a week.

After about the third week, the big red wagon appeared. This was a beautiful wagon. Karen spent about $300 to buy it. It had large rounded rubber wheels, a large bed to accommodate up to three angels, slatted wooden sides that were removable, and a long front handle for pulling. Karen took out the slatted side on the long right side, leaving three slatted sides, front, left and back to keep the angels in. The wagon could be pulled by up to two angels. Up to three angels could sit inside. They had to sit on their bottoms. Legs could not dangle. Hands could not touch the tires. No running while pulling the wagon. No pushing of the wagon from the back. The route of the wagon ran counterclockwise around the asphalt alphabet circle, stopping on the letter "H", where a line formed to take turns. A turn consisted of a two trips around the circle.

By the fourth week, Karen brought out a metal shopping cart filled with sand toys: dump trucks, steam shovels, loaders and hand tools; shovels, pails, trowels, and sifting implements. (Karen was always sending me to a local hardware store by to buy another half-dozen replacement hand trowels). The angels had to play cooperatively, share the toys and tools, quickly pick up the toys and tools, and return them to the shopping cart when Karen rang the sleigh bells to end recess. (The "ball" person for the week made sure that the final pick-up was complete).

Finally the tricycles were brought out, initially only one and soon all three. The rules were: travel counterclockwise, in the same direction, around the polygon-shaped cement walkway that bordered the sand-covered playground; keep a safe distance between you and the rider in front; no tailgating or bumping; keep the tricycle on the cement; a turn meant one complete trip around the playground; stop at the corner where the asphalt met the grass, get off if someone was waiting, and a new rider would begin his/her turn; otherwise ride until someone is waiting.

In the opening hours and days, every one of the above rules would be broken, repeatedly, and every time Karen would give a time out, and if a second offense occurred, that angel lost recess altogether. Soon the angels behaved, but the price of safe play was constant vigilance.

Karen never missed anything. She was hyper-vigilant, especially during those first six weeks.

If an angel brought a bracelet, or some such item, from home, which caused the angel to be constantly distracted, causing a lack of attention to the work of the class, Karen took it away until it was time to dismiss. Whenever an angel was distracted during an activity, Karen called them back to task.

If two angels were talking too much while sitting next to each other and it was becoming a distraction, Karen quickly changed the seating chart, separating the two. (Karen changed the seating arrangement four times per year, anyway).

Karen was extremely sensitive to disabilities and deficits. The disabled angels were always mainstreamed into Karen's kindergarten

Early one year a boy angel complained to me that his teeth hurt. I told Karen. She found a private moment and peered into the boy's mouth. Most of his baby teeth were rotten. She immediately called the school nurse, who found a dentist who would do the work for free, and made an appointment. The boy's indifferent parents missed the first several appointments, but Karen and the nurse kept the pressure on and a school year later, his teeth were fixed. Karen and the nurse did such things routinely.

If a child confided in Karen, or Karen noticed troubling behavior, she fought for an appointment with the school psychologist, or the speech therapist.

Karen sent me several times during the year to K-Mart to purchase about eight pairs of kindergarten-sized underwear for both boys and girls, and eight pairs of unisex jeans. So when the angels had potty accidents, she could quickly get them cleaned up and into dry clothes, and the soiled clothes went home that same day in a plastic bag. I don't remember a parent ever returning the new, free clothing.

Karen truly understood kindergartners. Once I was on the playground with Karen. I noted a boy on the swings and mentioned what a good reader he was, and how mature he seemed to be. "Yes," said Karen, "but he does not play well with his peers. I'm starting to pair him with another boy (whom she named) for recess time." I had never noticed.

Earlier, in the chapter **A BRILLIANT SMILE**, I explained that Karen could speak Kindergartenease. With her vast experience, she could decipher the most garbled speech. This inured to the benefit of the angels with speech problems, for they were much less frustrated, because they could communicate with Karen.

In the earlier chapter "**THE "G' WORD",** I noted how Karen taught the angels to be assertive in their personal relationships.

If an angel was in peril, Karen reported immediately to CWS. If CWS did not act fast enough, she called the Grover Beach Police Department. (Karen once upset CWS when, after she had called them after seeing strangulation marks on a girl angel's neck and they did not come, she called the police. Eventually, she had to testify in court against the parents, who went to jail).

Karen always paid out of her own pocket whatever money was necessary to enable the angels to go on field trips, as many of the parents could not afford even modest costs.

Karen could tell when the angels were too hyped to pay attention. Karen kept five different angels each weekday after school for tutoring from 12:30 to 1:25 p.m. So twenty-five angels would get this special time with Karen each week. The angels craved this time with Karen. One day, as the last of the angels dismissed at 12:30 were picked up, she turned to the pink center where the five boys she was about to tutor were supposed to be quietly playing with number puzzles. They were anything but quiet. It was a windy day, so Karen opened the back/north door onto the playground.

She called to the five boys. "Come here." They rushed to the doorway. "See that fence at the far end of the grass?"

"Yep," said the boys.

"Okay, run to it and run back." Off like buckshot, they sprinted in a tight group all the way out and all the way back, smiling from ear to ear.

Finding them insufficiently winded, Karen then said: "Okay, do it again." Off they shot again, although with a little less élan than before. When they returned, very winded, Karen had them go get a drink, wash their hands and faces, than arranged them at the red center where they had a relaxed and productive 25 minutes with word and number puzzles

Karen controlled the class in such a consistent, positive, and loving way, that the angels knew that she cared deeply for them, and she never played favorites. As a result, Karen was the focal point for all the angels. It was her presence and her approval that they constantly craved.

I could, and did, often spend a full half hour with an angel, finishing a project, but no matter how much I praised the angel and the work, they raced from the table to get Karen's approval, showing her their completed work. Without her attention and approval, they were not complete.

I never saw another teacher, or aide, watch over their angels as effectively as Karen. This was often apparent on the playground, when Karen's class had to interact with the kids from the other two kindergarten classes, who too often did not follow the playground rules, causing safety issues. Why did others let safety slide? It was easier not to keep the angels on track. It took constant vigilance and was quite stressful to keep them on track. But Karen expended the energy, right up to and through her last day of teaching.

Karen kept her high standards and the angels benefited. The classroom was quieter, safer, and more conducive to learning. And although the angels could not articulate it, they appreciated the safety of those boundaries. That is why when Karen took her angels to another location, or a new person visited Room 1, the angels always heard how "well behaved" they were.

One clever ploy that Karen sometimes used, when she needed the angels to be especially quiet when they traveled elsewhere on campus, was to have them imagine putting a wad of imaginary gum in their mouths and chewing it until arriving at their destination.

Karen always told the angels they would go to 1st grade, finish 6th grade, then go to middle school, then high school, and finally to college.

Once, Karen took the angels on two busses on an October field trip to the Cal Poly pumpkin patch in San Luis Obispo. Karen was in the lead bus, directing the driver. I followed in the second bus. The most direct route was to take HWY 1 to Highland, then turn right into Cal Poly, and turn the first left towards the pumpkin field. I was upset when Karen apparently directed the lead bus driver to go up Grand Avenue, through the heart of the Cal Poly campus, a much slower route.

I assumed Karen was lost. Karen has a limited sense of direction, about which I constantly tease her. A typical exchange, with Karen at the wheel, would be:

Karen: "I think I should turn left here."

Me, (in my smart ass lawyer persona): "Well, you could do that, but eventually you would arrive at the Jersey shore, gazing at the Atlantic Ocean, when if you turned right, in about two miles, you will be at your destination, gazing upon the Pacific Ocean."

This has happened so often that I refer to Karen as "Wing Commander Karen." I imagine her, leading a wing of bombers, speaking into her cockpit radio, saying: "Just follow me in boys and drop your bombs where I do." Thus blowing to bits a friendly field hospital, or a battalion of her own troops.

So when the busses eventually reached the pumpkin patch and we all alighted, I went up to Karen and asked, impatiently, why she went so far out of the way.

"I was showing the angels a college campus, telling them that someday they could go to college there."

Karen lived for the angels. Her thoughts were always on the angels and Room 1. Whenever we went into a homey mom and pop bookstore, or entered a bland corporate box, like a Barnes and Noble, or a Borders, Karen always went directly to the children's section, while I languished in the history, or wallowed in the poetry, sections. Karen always left with children's books. That is partly why she had over 1,500 volumes for the angels in Room 1.

In all this, Karen was so upbeat, so positive, so concerned about her angels, so utterly competent and committed to teaching them, that they all knew, from the first day, that she loved them.

Here is an example of Carl and Karen together at work.

On a long ago opening day, Carl and Karen had 33 kids in the morning session from and 8:30 a.m. to noon, and 33 more kids in the afternoon session from 11:00 to 2:30 p.m.

Thus, both sessions overlapped from 11:00 to noon, and all 66 kids were to be present.

At about 11:10 a.m., as 65 kids were on the rug being entertained by Karen, a late arriving boy entered with his mother. Clinging to his mother's right leg, the boy started screaming as she dragged him towards Carl.

"I hate you . . . I hate this place . . . I'm not going . . . I hate kindergarten . . ."

With Carl's help, the embarrassed mother pried her little boy away and into Carl's arms, who took the boy over onto the edge of the rug, away from the other 65 angels, who looked quizzically at the little boy as he continued his diatribe, while struggling in Carl's arms.

"I hate you . . . I hate this place . . . I won't stay here . . . I hate kindergarten . . . I hate . . . (now red faced, he paused for breath) . . . I don't want to be here . . . I want to go (pausing again for breath) home . . . I . . . (pausing again for breath) . . . I don't want to (pausing again for breath) . . . be here . . ." Red faced and breathless, he finally stopped.

After a decent interval, Carl looked down at the now silent boy and in a sweet soft voice said: "I'm sorry you feel that way, because . . . we . . . love . . . you."

The red color drained from the boy's face as he looked up at Carl. Now suddenly off balance, he became peaceful and at ease. After that moment, he never again had a rampage, became a model angel, and thrived in kindergarten.

Mrs. Brown "Gets A Tire"

By mid-September of 2010, Karen had announced to many, including the parents who attended Back to School Night, that she was in her final academic year of teaching and would retire in June of 2011.

A week after Back to School Night, on a Tuesday, a mid-morning fire drill was held, the first of the new school year. Karen and her class marched double file onto the expansive playgrounds on the south side of campus, joining the ranks formed by the rest of the student body, and awaited Mr. Olivarria's announcement through his bullhorn to return to class.

While waiting on the grass, Karen thought she heard one of her diminutive girl angels say something about "a tire."

Leaning down, she asked the girl angel if she had said "a tire."

The little angel's response was a question, "Mrs. Brown, are you going to get a tire?"

Momentarily confused, Karen asked the angel, "What do you mean 'get a tire'?"

The girl angel said, "It's when you don't work no more."

"Oh, honey, that's right. When I RETIRE, I will not be teaching anymore," explained Karen.

The Last Back To School Night

Karen's 37th and final Back to School Night commenced early in September of 2010.

Karen had prepared her classroom with her usual meticulous care, including sweeping the floor. When the maintenance lady appeared, she thanked Karen profusely for having swept the floor for her. "Nobody else does this for me," she said.

It was a festive affair on a beautiful evening.

The father of a student, who owned a portable catering business, had parked his red and white food trailer on a diamond-shaped wedge of grass just south of the main office and behind the cafeteria, where fajitas and hot dogs, condiments and cold drinks were prepared and served, commencing at 5:30 p.m.

The freshly mowed lawn gave off an emerald sheen beneath a cloudless turquoise sky. The golden rays of the sinking sun gave a lunar aspect to all. Lively mariachi music drifted from a boom box. A hot pint Frisbee veered in the air, tossed back and forth between two boisterous boys. Families arrayed themselves on blankets. Young couples with strollers lazily walked by. From a cobalt blue metal table outside room 10, Grover Beach Gopher T-shirts, all in navy blue, sold briskly.

Just before the program was to start, little Amaya, smiling broadly, displaying her missing, two upper-front teeth, ran out of the back door of the cafeteria, arms outstretched, to where I was standing to give me a hug. An indelible moment.

By 6:30 p.m. the parents assembled in the cafeteria so Mr. Oliviarra, a wonderful principal, could welcome them all to the new school year. After his brief remarks, the parents were to go to their child's classrooms. To accommodate those parents with students in two different grades, identical presentations would be made by the classroom teachers, the first session from 7:00 p.m. to 7:30 p.m. and the second from 7:30 p.m. to 8:00 p.m.

Mr. Olivarria introduced the teachers. When he introduced Karen, the room erupted in cheers and continued as all rose to give her a standing ovation.

I went with Karen back to Room 1 to await the arrival of the parents. They came in, signed in, and received a lovely eight-page handout. Karen went over each page.

She told the parents the daily kindergarten schedule; parent-teacher conference dates; the backpack rules (free ones available); when sharing times occurred; the need to label everything belonging to your child; all about snack breaks; exact school hours; the daily class schedule on a single page entitled "A Day in the Life of a Kindergartener;" about homework (the folder, worksheets) and math expectations; reading expectations; the importance of the angels printing their own names in D'Nealian style (with a separate two-page handout of the D'Nealian alphabet and an explanation of how to form each letter); the date for picture day, October 11, and what to wear; parent volunteer rules regarding TB testing (with handout) and fingerprinting (with handout); a listing of minimum days for the entire academic year; the trimester ending date of November 10; the health screening dates; and the importance of Zoo-phonics (with a three-page handout showing the animal for each letter and the physical movements associated with each).

I had seen Karen do this now for three years running. I continued to be amazed at her élan, that she still had such zest for her work. She glowed during her entire presentation. From time to time, I glanced around the room. Every adult was smiling continuously back at Karen, warmed by her presence.

At the break, many former students, now in the upper grades, and their parents stopped by to see Karen. There were hugs and smiles all around. When Karen hugged her former angels, they lit up like hundred-watt bulbs.

After the second presentation, more former students stopped by—hugs and smiles all around.

It was getting quite late. Karen eventually had to call an end to it so she could go home.

A Final Evaluation

Just a year before he ended his 36-year career, in June of 2012, with the Lucia Mar Unified School District, 26 of those years as a grade school principal, Juan Olivarria, Karen's superlative principal, wrote a final evaluation of Karen.

"Karen Brown has been teaching 36 years in the Lucia Mar Unified School District. This is her final year teaching in the classroom, after an incredible career. I can not describe the impact that her caring, nurturing, and effective teaching has made on generations of children. Another Kindergarten teacher will be in Room 1 next year, but Mrs. Karen Brown will never be replaced.

Karen Brown is a master at creating an effective, exciting and meaningful learning environment for her students. So many of the children attending Grover Beach School, unfortunately, come from homes where stability is lacking. The majority of children are from single parent households, where the family survives at the poverty level. Many of the single parents struggle to keep basic necessities available for their children, such as food and clothing. When the children enter Kindergarten many are damaged little souls whose only stability in their young lives has been the constant turmoil in which they live. Then the fortunate ones encounter Mrs. Karen Brown as their Kindergarten Teacher. Karen treats each and every child as if they were her own.

It doesn't matter what the needs are for the child, Karen dedicates herself to helping each child. As stated, Karen is a master at creating an effective and safe learning environment. Her classroom is always, and I mean always, a happy environment where children learn to love school. Karen respects each child, and their families, by being non-judgmental, but, becoming an advocate for the child. Children in Karen's classroom learn to respect and care for each other, to develop their academic skills, to be responsible, and to have high aspirations in life. I have known and observed many Kindergarten Teachers, many who have been outstanding. Mrs. Karen Brown is at the pinnacle of our profession. She is the 'gold standard' on being a teacher."[61]

Principal Juan Olivarria

[61]   Juan Olivarria, *Certificated Evaluation*, (January 27, 2011).

Retirement Parties

About two weeks before Karen retired, the Grover Beach staff held a lovely party for her at the elegant Dolphin Bay resort in Shell Beach. The 50 participants each directed kind words to Karen, and presented her with a unique charm and a new charm bracelet.

But Karen also wanted a chance to say goodbye to all former students and their parents, so a retirement party for the general public was set on Saturday, June 4th, at the Mentone Street Park in Grover Beach, just two days before the commencement of Karen's final week of teaching,

The event had been well publicized in our local newspapers.

On the appointed day, Karen's fellow kindergarten teachers had prepared 400 cupcakes and arranged them upon the six picnic tables under the corner picnic area covered by a pole roof. Good thing, because June 4, 2011 turned into a windy, rainy day. Normally, from June1 to September 1, a single cloud is an event and rain is totally unexpected.

Despite the weather, about 100 people came, including some children, along with former Grover Beach staff and old friends.

RETIREMENT PICNIC

Honoring Karen Woodward Brown, who is retiring after 36 years of teaching Kindergarten in Room #1 at Grover Beach Elementary School. All current and former: students and their families, faculty, staff, friends and well wishers are invited.

Saturday, June 4, 2011
Noon to 3:00 PM.
16th Street Park,
16th & Mentone,
Grover Beach,
California.

BYO: lunch/non-alcoholic drinks.
Dessert provided.

Karen's public Retirement Picnic announcement

I noticed one visitor who stayed for the entire rainy event. It was a mature seagull, totally white, except for his orange beak. He behaved like an observer. Strangely, he did not swoop in to get crumbs from the cupcakes. When little kids chased him away, he just flew out of range and returned after they had left. After the party ended, and all the plastic cups and plastic tablecloths had been thrown into the trash, only then did the gull lift off, make one pass back over Karen, and soared out of sight. I wondered if it was one of Pavlov's gulls, giving a final salute to Karen.

A Swinger Of Angels

The familiar olive-skinned face of a little girl angel, representing a small group, looked up expectantly at me, as she asked her familiar question: "Meester Brown, would you pooch us?"

That was the Spanish inflected version of the question I was most often asked when the angels went out onto the playground. At recess, as soon as I stepped outside the classroom door, the allure of the question awaited.

"Sure," I would always say. "I'll meet you over at the swings." And the gaggle of little girls sprinted toward the swings.

The colorful swings were almost new and solidly made. Four parallel vertical posts anchored in cement, coated with hard plastic, colored cobalt blue, supported a horizontal connecting bar in canary yellow, forming three parallel rectangles, each containing two swings. Each swing consisted of two parallel links of heavy chain, bolted to the canary yellow cross bar at the top, separated by an 18" arc of smooth rubber forming a seat at the bottom.

I was the swinger.

I swung the angels high. At my height, when I pulled the swing back for the first push, the little angel was already four feet above the ground. I then let go with a hard push and followed with two softer pushes until the angel had achieved altitude.

It was never enough. "Higher . . . higher," I always heard.

I sometimes did other things. I briefly pulled the angels in the large red wagon around the alphabet circle on the asphalt outside the classroom door. I tossed a rubber ball or bounced a basketball, mostly with the boys, but often with girls. But these were mere preludes to the swinging.

The swinging was the thing. I was in great and constant demand. I finally had to limit the angels to two turns each, or others would never get a turn.

The angels loved the fresh air, the sparkling sun, the brief interval of weightlessness at the top of the pendulum, and the accelerating rush as gravity asserted its familiar downward pull.

In the poem "*Birches*", Robert Frost writes about the joy of boys swinging on the supple limbs of New England birch trees, climbing almost to the top, toward heaven, then leaning out as the branch bends down and deposits the boy onto the ground, back to earth.

He concludes:

> "I'd like to go by climbing a birch tree,
> And climb black branches up a snow-white trunk
> *Toward* heaven, till the tree could bear no more,
> But dipped its top and set me down again.
> That would be good both going and coming back.
> One could do worse than be a swinger of birches."[62]

In this life, one could do no better than to be a swinger of angels.

---

[62] Robert Frost, *The Poetry Of Robert Frost, The Collected Poems*, Edited by Edward Connery Lathem, P. 122, Holt Paperbacks, Henry Holt and Company (1969).

A Last Letter

Karen and Carl composed this poem, which always went home to the parents on the final day of school.

Dear Parents,

I've worked with your flower,
And helped it to grow.
I'm returning it now
But I want you to know . . .
This flower is precious,
As dear as can be,
Love it: take care of it,
And then you will see
A bright new bloom with every day.
It grows and blossoms in such wonderful ways,
In September a bud, January a bloom,
Now a lovely blossom I return to you in June.
Remember this flower and what it will be,
Thanks mostly to you, And a little to me![63]

Karen Brown
Kindergarten 2010-2011

---

[63] Both Karen and Carl always signed the poem, but after Carl's death in 2004, only Karen signed.

The Dress

So accomplished was Karen's mother, Dolores, as a seamstress, that as a young woman she made bespoke clothing for private customers in Cleveland, her home town. After she married her husband, Joe, Dolores also hand tailored clothing for each of her four children.

So it was a natural that in the spring of her first year in kindergarten, and for 35 springs thereafter, Karen turned to Dolores to tailor "The Dress."

The Dress consisted of 5" by 7" squares, each colored by an angel, which had been cut out and sewn into a jumper pattern by Dolores. The Dress fit Karen like a glove, because Dolores was such a good tailor.

Karen commenced the process by purchasing three yards of smooth cotton cloth, usually white, but sometimes in pastels of pink, yellow, blue, and green. She then made a pattern on the cloth, creating 40 rectangles, each 5" by 7".

Karen would place the roll of cloth at the pink center, controlled by Irene, and explain to the angels that they were making a dress for Mrs. Brown to wear at Open House night. Each angel was to draw a picture, or some design, using permanent marker pens, onto two rectangles, and then Mrs. Brown's mother would select the best rectangle from each angel and sew the rectangles into The Dress.

The angels loved this project. When finished, and Karen first wore The Dress, the angels would crowd around Karen at Open House night and show their parents which rectangle they had created.

After Open House night, Karen wore The Dress once a week until the end of school, and always on the last day of school.

Karen has kept all of her cherished kindergarten dresses stored in boxes in our garage. She models one on the cover of this book.

Sadly, for Karen's last two years, Dolores could not sew The Dress because of arthritis on her hands and fingers.

I have indelible memories of Karen on the last day of school standing just outside the south doorway of Room 1, on the edge of the playground, saying goodbye, hugging the angels and their parents, with various angels clinging to The Dress.

The Last Day

Friday June 10th, 2011, marked Karen's final day in kindergarten, the 180th school day of the 2010-2011academic year.

Karen had been preparing the angels for this day.

Together that had been counting the days of school from day one. Before the school year started, beneath the letters of the alphabet and the Zoo-phonics characters, Karen had stretched a narrow strip of white paper. On the first day of school, she wrote a number one on the strip of paper.

Every day thereafter, after the opening song, the weather, the calendar, the flag salute, and the writing of a sentence, Karen had asked the angels to name the next number to write onto the white strip of paper, as she counted the days the angels had been in school. After the angels got to number 150, Karen would tell the angels that when the days got to 180, that would be the last day of school.

And on this day, after the opening song, the weather, the calendar, the flag salute, and the writing of a sentence, Karen wrote the final number, 180, onto the white strip of paper and again told the angels this was the last day of kindergarten, and they would next move on the 1st grade.

For months Karen had been telling the angels that their next grade would be 1ˢᵗ grade. After the Spring Open House, Karen had taken the angels to visit a first-grade classroom.

After the familiar class opening events, Karen and the other kindergarten teachers had planned a morning of outdoor fun for the angels. The last day was a shortened day, which ended at noon. So the angels were going to play outside from 9:00 a.m. to 10:00 a.m., eat lunch at 10:00 a.m., play till 11:30 a.m., then have a few final minutes in class and leave at noon.

Outside on the kindergarten playground, 10 activity stations awaited. The angels moved gleefully from the Bean Bag Toss; to the Ring Toss; to the Jump Rope station; to the Water Table; to the Bowling Lane; to the Parachute; to the Chalk Circle; to the Hula Hoops; to Hop Scotch, and to the Playground Equipment (swings, slides, jungle gyms, teeter totter, and the climbing wall).

After lunch, when the angels had returned to resume their play stations, I was inside the Room1, between the red and pink center tables, talking briefly with Karen, when Sierra walked in. I will always remember Sierra: brown haired, bright eyed, flashing an infectious smile, always hugging everyone, even me.

She walked up to Karen and hugged her. Then she stepped back and with a concerned expression, looked up and asked: "Mrs. Brown, what does the last day mean?"

"Well," said Karen, "it means starting this afternoon, you will enjoy a fun summer break, a vacation, but when you come back at the end of the summer, you will be in a new room, a 1st grade room, but you will be with many of your friends from this class."

Continuing to hug Karen, Sierra broke into tears: "I don't want to go to first grade. I want to stay here with you."

Karen continued to hug Sierra: "I will be here on campus to see you next fall when you come back. Even though I am retiring and won't be in Room 1 anymore, I will be back often and I will see you often."

Tears began to form in my own eyes as I helplessly watched Karen and Sierra. After an interval Sierra retuned to the playground and resumed play.

At 11:30 the angels came into the room, along with some parents, and for much of the next half hour Karen opened presents, which she always made into an entertaining guessing game. She would hold up the wrapped gift, gently shake it and look at it from all angles, while asking the angels to confirm her implausible guesses.

Taking up a small box, Karen looks at the angels arrayed before her on the rug and said: "Do you think it's an elephant?"

"Noooooooooooooooo," shrieked the angels.

Karen then said: "I'll bet it's a peanut butter sandwich."

"Noooooooooooooo," sang the angels.

Finally Karen opened the box to find a small ceramic owl. Karen cooed over the owl. "This is the best present ever." Showing it to the angels, she said: "This is so beautiful. I just love this. Thank you so much_____, for this beautiful gift." The little angel who had given the gift was transfixed with happiness at Karen's reaction.

This process repeated itself over and over again until finally it was time to sing the "Goodbye Song" for one last time. That done, Karen hugged every angel one last time and the angels left Room 1, well prepared for the future and 1st grade.

After the angels and their caregivers had gone, a score of former parents and former students, staff and friends stopped to pay their respects. After they had gone, Karen and Irene exchanged a long embrace near the cubbies. True to her word, Irene had been at Karen's side from the day after Carl's memorial service until the day Karen retired, seven years later. A true and noble friend.

Karen never relaxed her standards. She had complete control of the class, the angels at rapt attention, hanging on her every word and gesture. Even on the final day, she had to put one girl angel into a brief time out. She kept the angels moving, engaged in the tasks at hand, safe and secure, and knowing they were mightily loved.

In August, when the new school year commenced, Karen volunteered in kindergarten classrooms every Tuesday, and sometime more often. Early in September I accompanied her. It was a break time and Karen was in the teachers' room near the 1st grade classrooms. As Karen emerged from the teachers' room, Sierra came running out of her classroom to hug Karen. It was a happy reunion.

Sierra was immediately joined by a crush of other angels from her former kindergarten class. All hugged Karen. Some, including Sierra, even hugged me.

A Memorial

Karen and Carl always intended to retire together. Carl was about five years older than Karen. On the date that Carl died in November of 2004, he had already been eligible to retire from teaching and was financially secure, but he had decided to wait until Karen could retire, so they could go out together.

After the memorial bench was dedicated to Carl on the edge of the kindergarten playground, Karen wanted, upon her retirement, to have a bench dedicated to her to be placed next to Carl's bench.

Principal Juan Olivarria readily agreed and he solicited donations from faculty and staff. I guaranteed the basic cost.

In early September of 2011, just a few months after Karen formally retired, a dedication was held on the kindergarten playground.

It was a fitting assembly that morning. The angels from all three kindergarten classes and all three 1st grade classes, about 120 all, along with their teachers and aides, were present. They waited on the asphalt behind the benches. Irene Gonzalez graced the gathering by her presence.

Though the sun hid behind a bank of high fog that blanketed the school, I have never seen Karen more animated. She beamed with happiness at seeing her former angels and former colleagues, especially Jaime Tucker and Irene. As the 1st graders came around the corner onto the playground, many burst from the ranks to hug Karen. Karen hugged everybody.

Juan gave a short sweet speech, telling the angels that though Mrs. Brown had just retired and would no longer be teaching in Room 1, she had made such an important contribution to Grover Beach Elementary, that she was being honored permanently with a bench, placed right next to that of her dear friend and fellow teacher, Mr. Daughters, with whom she team taught kindergarten for 25 years.

Karen then spoke a few sentences. She said it had been an honor to have been a kindergarten teacher at Grover Beach Elementary. She had loved every minute of it, especially the children, the little angels in her care, and that she would be back often to volunteer in kindergarten.

Then it was time to unveil the bench. It had been draped with a green checkered blanket that displayed on the front, eight handwritten notes inscribed within pink and red hearts: saying such things as: "Mrs. Brown, we love you and miss you-Grover Beach School"; "Mrs. Brown, we love you-from the 5th grade"; and "We Love you."

Juan then pulled off the blanket to reveal the brown metal bench set in cement in perfect alignment with Carl's green metal bench. Cut out of the back of the bench were the words: "MRS BROWN".

Karen then sat upon the bench for the most fitting tribute of all—the parade of the angels. As they walked past Karen, they paid their respects and then continued around the polygon shaped sidewalk that enclosed the playground equipment and returned to their classrooms.

Ever the teacher, Karen would ask about every third angel: "What color is this bench?" or, "What letter am I pointing to?"

Many stopped to hug her, especially from her last class. Some had tears in their eyes, and so did I.

Juan and Karen bookend Karen's
Memorial Bench, just after the parade of angels had ended.

After six years have passed, no angels taught by Karen will remain at Grover Beach Elementary. Karen will be unknown to the new flights of angels. But sometime in the future, someone will look at Karen's bench and ask: "Who was MRS. BROWN?"

These pages try to answer that question and will, I hope, provide to Karen (and Carl and Irene and the angels) a small, yet Shakespearean, immortality:

> "Or I shall live your epitaph to make,
> Or you survive when I in earth am rotten,
> From hence your memory death cannot take,
> Although in me each part will be forgotten.
> Your name from hence immortal life shall have,
> Though I, once gone, to all the world must die;
> The earth can yield me but a common grave
> When you entombed in men's eyes shall lie.
> Your monument shall be my gentle verse,
> Which eyes not yet created shall o'er-read,
> And tongues to be your being shall rehearse
> When all the breathers of this world are dead:
> You still shall live (such virtue hath my pen)
> Where breath most breathes, even in the mouths of men." [64]

---

[64] William Shakespeare, *Sonnets*, Edited by Barbara Herrnstein Smith, Sonnet 81, p.135, Avon Books and New York University Press (1969).

A Big Heart

Many years ago, the fifth graders wrote their own play, which they performed in the cafeteria the night of Open House in front of hundreds of parents and staff.

The play depicted various teachers on the staff and also the custodian.

They aptly depicted the custodian as a big, boisterous man with a playful nature, teasing the older kids a lot and singing Elvis Presley songs over the loudspeaker.

A fifth-grade actor who walked through the audience picking up pre-positioned trash played the principal, who often picked up trash from the playgrounds.

One of Karen's former students, a lovely girl, depicted "Mrs. Brown." For a costume, she wore a white dress with a gigantic red heart painted on her chest.

Throughout the play, "Mrs. Brown" went from one character to another, hugging them and saying, "There, there now, everything is going to be all right," and "Let me help you with that, sweetheart."

During the 17 years that Karen told me stories from kindergarten, this was the only story that, in the telling, reduced her to tears.

The Archangel

In the winter of her last year, Karen became sufficiently ill that even she stayed home and actually missed three days of school.

I accompanied her on her return. I wanted to witness the angels' reactions. When she walked onto campus, she came upon the open cafeteria door and poked her head in.

The first two tables were filled with her students. They shrieked with delight and scrambled *en masse* from their tables to run to embrace her.

It was then that I had an epiphany. Karen is an archangel.

She was put on this earth to take the little angels unto her, to shelter them in a safe place, to teach them the colors of the rainbow, the music of the spheres, the shapes of things, the sounds made by the letters of the alphabet, to sound out words, to read, to count, to know the days of the week, the months of the year, to sing, to dance, to play, to swing, to take turns, to flush and to love one another.

Each moment she spent in Room 1 with the angels, she was in a state of grace.

When Karen dies the world will sigh. If I am then alive, at her memorial service, after relating the events of her lovely life, I will say:

"Goodnight, sweet princess.
Flights angels will sing you to your rest,
Out among the circling stars,
And confer upon you your crown,
And it will be a constellation."

Acknowledgements

My thanks to:

Webster's New World Dictionary of the American Language, College Edition, published in 1966. For sentimental reasons, I typed this manuscript in Word Perfect format on an old PC that Carl Daughters had assembled for me over 15 year ago. But the Word Perfect program had a hitch I never fixed, which caused me to lose the document if I attempted to employ spell check. Thus, my faithful reliance upon Noah Webster.

The generosity and skill of my former wife, Johanna Billingsley Brown, librarian emeritus, who located a host of obscure volumes, so I could quote from them, and for introducing me to that superlative reference work, *The Chicago Manual Of Style.*

Virginia Hiramatsu of ACES Transcribing and Secretarial Services of Morro Bay, California, for converting the entire text from Word Perfect to Microsoft Word.

Juan Olivarria, the just-retired superb principal of Grover Beach Elementary. Juan provided valuable background information and reviewed, at my request, drafts of the chapters entitled: "Grover Beach" and "Grover Beach Elementary."

Irene Gonzalez for allowing me to interview her about her life, and for her faithfulness to Karen and to the angels, especially after Carl Daughters died.

Gail Piedalue of Piedalue Productions for: putting the photographs into proper format; arranging captions for the Room 1 photo and the HEP Stacks photo; providing the front and back cover photographs, photos of Karen's and Carl's memorial benches and "Karate Karen."

The angels for allowing me to come into Room 1, to experience kindergarten along with them, and for lending to my life a peace I had never known.

And Karen—for everything.

Photo Credits

All photographs are by the author, except for those taken by Gail Piedalue: the front and back cover, Karen's bench, Carl's bench and "Karate Karen."

The head shots of Karen, Carl and Irene that appear on the single-paged papers entitled "I'm A Kindergarten Star," appearing opposite the chapters entitled "Karen", "Carl", and "Irene," were taken with Karen's camera, sometime in the 1980's. Carl took the photos of Karen and Irene. Karen took the photo of Carl and the head shot of me.